SINGER
SEWING REFERENCE LIBRARY

Designer Projects
for BED&BATH

CREATIVE
PUBLISHING
international

President: Iain Macfarlane
Group Director, Book Development: Zoe Graul
Creative Director: Lisa Rosenthal
Executive Managing Editor: Elaine Perry

DESIGNER PROJECTS FOR BED & BATH

Created by: The Editors of Creative Publishing international,
Inc., in cooperation with the Sewing Education
Department, Singer Sewing Company. Singer is a trade-
mark of The Singer Company Limited and is used under
license.

Senior Editor: Linda Neubauer
Project Manager: Jill Anderson
Senior Art Director: Mark Jacobson
Copy Editor: Janice Cauley
Mac Design Manager: Jon Simpson
Desktop Publishing Specialist: Laurie Kristensen
Lead Project & Prop Stylist: Joanne Wawra
Project Stylists: Christine Jahns, Coralie Sathre
Sample Production Manager: Elizabeth Reichow
Lead Samplemaker: Phyllis Galbraith
Samplemakers: Arlene Dohrman, Sheila Duffy, Sharon
Eklund, Bridget Haugh, Muriel Lynch, Virginia Mateen,
Delores Minkema
Senior Technical Photo Stylist: Bridget Haugh
Technical Photo Stylists: Jennifer Bailey, Sharon Eklund
Studio Services Manager: Marcia Chambers
Photo Services Coordinator: Carol Osterhus
Senior Lead Photographer: Chuck Nields
Photographers: Tate Carlson, Andrea Rugg
Scene Shop Carpenter: Dan Widerski
Manager, Production Services: Kim Gerber
Production Staff: Curt Ellering, Laura Hokkanen, Kay
Wethern

Contributors:
American Olean Tile Company; Andersen Windows, Inc.;
Armstrong Flooring; Calico Corners Decorative Fabrics;
Coats & Clark Inc.; Conso Products Company; Creative
Home Textiles/Mill Creek; Dritz Corporation; Dyno
Merchandise Corporation; EZ International; Fabby
Custom Lighting; Formica Corp.; General Marble; Graber
Industries, Inc; HTC-Handler Textile Corporation; Keith
Raivo Designs; Kirsch Division, Cooper Industries, Inc.;
Laces & Lacemaking; Land o' Lace; Macy's; Plaid
Enterprises, Inc.; Scandia Down Shops; The Singer
Company; Spartex Inc.; Swiss-Metrosene, Inc.; Untapped
Resource—Sheryl Vanderpol; Waverly, Division of F.
Schumacher & Company; Windmill Imports, Inc.

Books available in this series:
*Sewing Essentials, Sewing for the Home, Clothing Care & Repair,
Sewing for Style, Sewing Specialty Fabrics, Sewing Activewear, The
Perfect Fit, Timesaving Sewing, More Sewing for the Home,
Tailoring, Sewing for Children, 101 Sewing Secrets, Sewing Pants
That Fit, Quilting by Machine, Decorative Machine Stitching,
Creative Sewing Ideas, Sewing Lingerie, Sewing Projects for the
Home, Sewing with Knits, More Creative Sewing Ideas, Quilt
Projects by Machine, Creating Fashion Accessories, Quick & Easy
Sewing Projects, Sewing for Special Occasions, Sewing for the
Holidays, Quick & Easy Decorating Projects, Quilted Projects &
Garments, Embellished Quilted Projects, Window Treatments,
Holiday Projects, Halloween Costumes, Upholstery Basics, The
New Sewing with a Serger, The New Quilting by Machine*

Printed on American paper by:
R. R. Donnelley & Sons Co.
02 01 00 99 / 5 4 3 2 1

Creative Publishing international, Inc. offers a variety of
how-to books. For information write:

Creative Publishing international, Inc.
Subscriber Books
5900 Green Oak Drive
Minnetonka, MN 55343

Library of Congress Cataloging-in-Publication Data

Designer projects for bed & bath. - - Designer projects for bed and bath.
p. cm. - - (Singer sewing reference library)
Includes index.
ISBN 0-86573-331-7 (hardcover). - - ISBN 0-86573-332-5 (soft cover)
1. Household linens. 2. House furnishings. 3. Textile fabrics in
interior decoration. 4. Machine sewing. I. Series.
TT387.D47 1999
646.2'1- -dc21   98-49789

SINGER
SEWING REFERENCE LIBRARY

Designer Projects
for BED & BATH

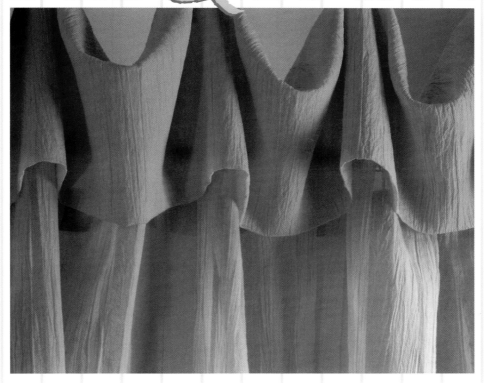

CREATIVE
PUBLISHING
international

Table of CONTENTS

Designer Projects for
BED & BATH

Wander through an upscale bed and bath shop, and you will find completely coordinated ensembles; sheets and pillowcases, duvets, shams, bed skirts, window treatments, and pillows, all made from coordinating fabrics. You'll also discover attractive designer detailing like welted seams, embroidered designs, appliqués, and unique closures, features that also add greatly to the cost of the ensembles. Decorator towels will beckon you with their luxurious softness and exquisite embellishments, though their prices may suggest they are not to be used.

Fortunately that designer look, with all the unique detailing, can be yours much more affordably, because you know how to sew! Each bedroom offers you a fresh blank palette to design as you wish, sewing window treatments and bedding ensembles to fit the personalities and preferences of the people who use them. Master bedroom and bathroom suites can be coordinated with matching window and shower curtains, fringed rugs, and personally accented towels and bed linens.

Delight your family and guests with an assortment of personal-touch accessories. Sew dreamy pillows to toss on the bed. Or sew a bedside caddy to keep reading material and personal amenities close at hand. Outfit a hamper with a convenient and colorful liner that doubles as a laundry bag. Add softness as well as storage space with a gathered sink or vanity skirt.

You can have the best of both worlds! Sewing for your bedrooms and bathrooms allows you to decorate creatively and extravagantly, with projects that are practical and easy on the budget.

Extravagant yet Affordable

High Style – Low Mainenance

Posh but Practical

Bedding BASICS

Make your own bedspreads, coverlets, duvet covers, bed skirts, and pillow shams to fit the decor of your bedroom. Mediumweight decorator fabrics, such as sateens, are good choices for bedding, because they are durable and drape well. Sheets may also be used; their width makes seaming unnecessary on some projects.

Whether the bed is a twin, full, queen, or king, the measurements will vary within each category, depending on the model or manufacturer. Measure the bed to make custom bed coverings and bed skirts that fit perfectly. Take the measurements over the blankets and sheets that will normally be used on the bed, to ensure that the bed covering will fit correctly. Measure the length of the bed from the head of the bed to the foot **(a),** and the width of the bed from side to side **(b).**

Duvets and coverlets reach 1" to 4" (2.5 to 10 cm) below the mattress on the sides and at the foot of the bed. Determine the drop length of the duvet or coverlet by measuring the distance from the top of the bed to the desired position for the lower edge of the duvet or coverlet **(c).** The drop length is usually 9" to 12" (23 to 30.5 cm), depending on the mattress depth.

When measuring for a full-length bedspread, measure the drop length from the top of the mattress to the floor **(d);** then subtract ½" (1.3 cm) for clearance.

When measuring for a bed skirt, measure the drop length from the top of the box spring to the floor **(e);** then subtract ½" (1.3 cm) for clearance.

Bed pillows also vary in size, depending on the amount of stuffing used. For best results, measure the bed pillow to determine the size of the pillow sham.

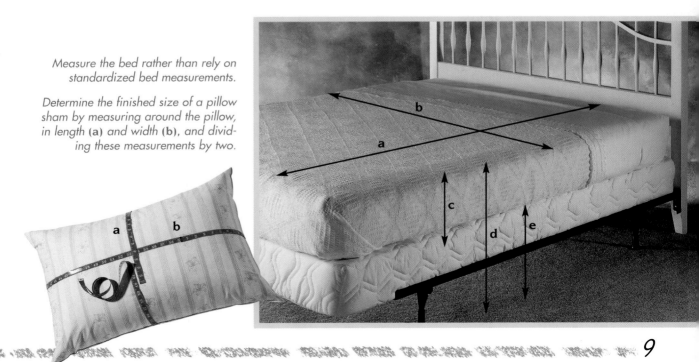

Measure the bed rather than rely on standardized bed measurements.

Determine the finished size of a pillow sham by measuring around the pillow, in length (a) and width (b), and dividing these measurements by two.

Bedspreads

The basic bedspread, unlined and hemmed on all sides, is the easiest bed covering to make. A full-length bedspread looks best when made from heavier fabric that drapes well, such as a damask or tapestry. A shorter, comforter-length bedspread, or coverlet, which is used with a bed skirt, can be made from a fabric that is lighter in weight. A variety of looks can be achieved using different trims along the lower edge of the bedspread.

Ruffles (above) are added to a bedspread for a traditional, romantic style.

Lace edging (above) is romantic and luxurious. Lace has also been topstitched over the seams on the bedspread for an added embellishment.

Twisted welting (below) is sewn to the edge of a bedspread to create a look that is tailored and elegant.

Bullion fringe (below) is elegantly traditional when used on a bedspread made from tapestry fabric.

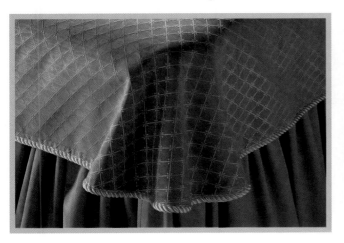

Making a
Basic Bedspread

1 Seam center and side panels, right sides together. Finish seam allowances by serging or zigzagging; press. Press under ½" (1.3 cm) along upper edge of bedspread; then press under 2" (5 cm).

2 Place the bedspread on the bed with equal drop length distributed on sides and foot of bed. Pin-mark one corner of bedspread along edge of mattress at foot of bed.

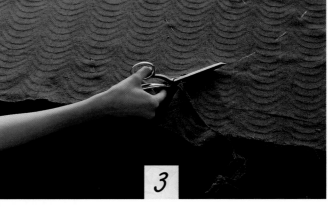

3 Fold the bedspread in half lengthwise; place on flat surface. Measure from pin marks in step 2 to desired finished drop length plus ½" (1.3 cm) hem allowance, at 2" to 3" (5 to 7.5 cm) intervals; mark with chalk. Cut through both layers of fabric to round lower corners.

4 Finish side and lower edges. Press under ½" (1.3 cm), and topstitch ⅜" (1 cm) from fold-line. Stitch hem at upper edge.

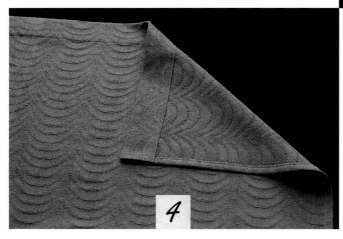

Making a
Bedspread
with a Ruffle

BEDSPREAD WITH WELTING, RUFFLE, FRINGE, OR LACE

WORKSHEET

Follow basic bedspread worksheet (opposite) to find cut length:
Subtract finished width of trim   − _____
to find adjusted cut length.   = _____

Follow basic bedspread worksheet to find cut width:
Subtract finished width of trim twice   − _____
to find adjusted cut width.   = _____

Add cut length twice   + _____
plus cut width   + _____
plus 2" (5 cm)   + 2" _____
to find length of trim needed.   = _____

1

1 Follow steps 1 to 3, opposite. Cut fabric strips for ruffle as on page 19, step 1. Make ruffle and apply it, with ends of ruffle at hemline, as on page 19, steps 2 to 4. Finish seam allowances by zigzagging or serging; press toward bedspread.

2 Stitch hem in place at upper edge. Topstitch along sides and lower edge, from right side, ³⁄₈" (1 cm) from seam, stitching through seam allowances. Machine-stitch or hand-stitch ends of hem.

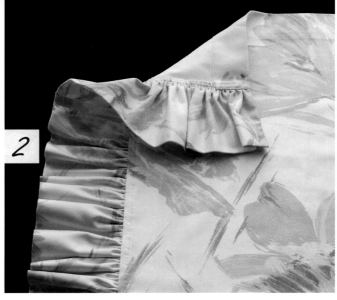

2

Making a **Bedspread with Twisted Welting**

1 Follow steps 1 to 3 on page 12; finish side and lower edges. Pin welting to right side of bedspread with welting ½" (1.3 cm) from raw edge and with ends extending 1" (2.5 cm) beyond hemline. Remove stitching from welting tape for about 1½" (3.8 cm) at ends. Untwist end of welting.

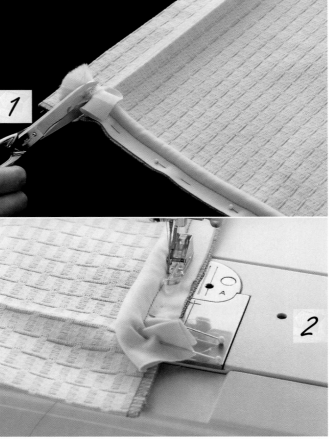

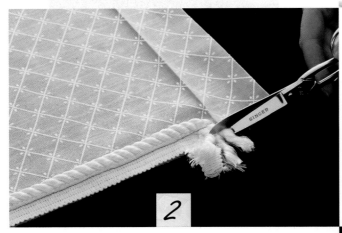

2 Curve welting into seam allowance; pin. Stitch welting to bedspread, ½" (1.3 cm) from raw edge, using zipper foot. Trim ends of welting. Press seam allowances toward bedspread.

3 Stitch hem in place at upper edge. Topstitch along sides and lower edge, from right side, ⅜" (1 cm) from seam, stitching through seam allowances. Machine-stitch or hand-stitch ends of hem.

Making a **Bedspread with Fabric Welting**

1 Follow steps 1 to 3 on page 12; finish side and lower edges. Cut enough bias welting strips to equal sides and lower edge of bedspread plus extra for piecing. Make welting, steps 1 and 2, page 20; pin to right side of bedspread, matching raw edges and with ends of welting extending 1" (2.5 cm) beyond hemline. Remove stitching from welting for 1" (2.5 cm) at ends; remove cording up to hemline.

2 Curve welting into seam allowance; pin. Stitch welting to bedspread, using zipper foot. Trim ends of welting. Press seam allowances toward bedspread. Finish as in step 3, above.

1 Follow steps 1 to 3 on page 12. Finish side and lower edges. Stitch hem at upper edge; pin trim on bedspread, right sides up, with end of trim extending 1" (2.5 cm) beyond hemmed edge and with upper edge of trim ½" (1.3 cm) from edge of bedspread. Pin in place up to curve of corner.

2 Ease the trim around rounded corner; steam to shape trim. If necessary, hand-stitch a row of gathering stitches through the heading of the trim to distribute fullness. Continue to pin trim to bedspread on the lower edge and remaining side, shaping the trim at remaining corner.

3 Stitch along inner edge of trim, using straight stitch or narrow zigzag stitch. Remove any gathering stitches.

4 Fold ends of trim under twice to wrong side of bedspread, making ½" (1.3 cm) double-fold hem; stitch. For sheer lace, seam allowance may be pressed toward bedspread and edgestitched before finishing ends.

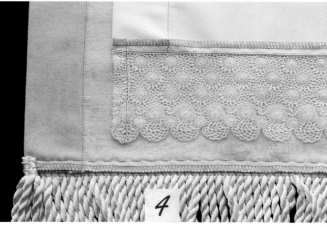

Duvet COVERS

A duvet cover keeps a duvet, or comforter, clean. Made from lightweight washable fabric or sheets, the duvet cover is easily removed for laundering. Frequently paired with bed skirts (page 23), duvet covers can be edged with welting for a tailored look, or bordered with ruffles for a romantic look.

This basic duvet style has a zipper closure concealed on the underside. Unless the duvet is made from sheets, the fabric must be pieced to the necessary width. One full width of fabric is used for a center panel and two equal, partial widths for side panels, for both the front and back.

MATERIALS

Lightweight, washable decorator fabric, sheeting, or batiste.

Two zippers, each 22" (56 cm) long, for zipper closure.

Cord, such as pearl cotton, for gathering ruffles; optional.

Cording, up to ¾" (2 cm) in diameter, to make welting; optional.

Welting (above and right, top and bottom) defines the edges of a duvet cover for a classic look.

Ruffles (top, right) give a duvet cover a more romantic, feminine look. They are attached only to the sides and lower edge of the cover. On the duvet cover shown, welting has also been added. First apply the welting to the duvet front; then apply the ruffle.

Tucked duvet cover (bottom, right) features lengthwise tucks on each side. The wide tucks add interest and detailing to the large expanse of fabric.

Making a
Basic Duvet Cover

1 Cut fabric for duvet cover front 1" (2.5 cm) wider and longer than the duvet. If piecing is necessary, use one full fabric width for center panel and two equal, partial widths for side panels. Cut fabric for back to same width as front, and 1½" (3.8 cm) shorter than front. Cut a zipper strip 3½" (9 cm) wide with length equal to cut width of back.

2 Finish upper edge of zipper strip and lower edge of duvet cover back. Press under finished edge of the zipper strip ½" (1.3 cm), and finished edge of the back 1" (2.5 cm).

3 Place closed zippers facedown on seam allowance of the back, with zipper tabs meeting in center and with edge of zipper tapes on fold. Using zipper foot, stitch along side of zippers nearest finished edge.

4 Turn right side up. Place pressed edge of zipper strip along edge of zipper teeth on other side of the zippers, and stitch close to edge. Backstitch at the end of zippers.

5 Stitch across end of one zipper; topstitch through all layers to stitch seam from zipper to side of cover. Repeat to stitch from other end of zipper to opposite side. Open zippers. Round lower corners, if desired, as on page 12, steps 2 and 3. (Contrasting thread was used to show detail.)

6 Pin duvet cover front to back, right sides together; stitch ½" (1.3 cm) seam on all sides. Turn right side out through zipper opening.

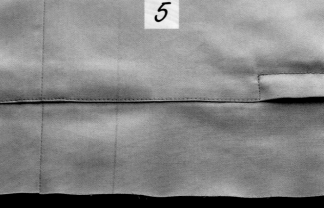

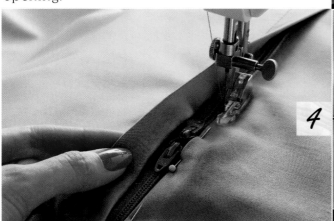

Making a
Duvet Cover with a Ruffle

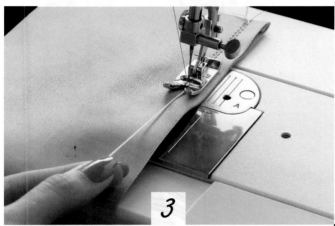

1 Follow steps 1 to 5 for the basic duvet cover (opposite). Cut fabric strips for ruffle on crosswise or lengthwise grain, with combined length of strips two to three times the distance to be ruffled. Ruffles are only attached to the sides and lower edge of a duvet cover. Width of strips is two times the finished width of ruffle plus 1" (2.5 cm) for seam allowances.

2 Stitch fabric strips for ruffle together in ¼" (6 mm) seams, right sides together. Fold pieced strip in half lengthwise, right sides together; stitch across ends in ¼" (6 mm) seams. Turn right side out; press ends and foldline.

3 Zigzag over cord a scant ½" (1.3 cm) from raw edges. For more control when adjusting gathers, zigzag over a second cord, within seam allowance, ¼" (6 mm) from first cord.

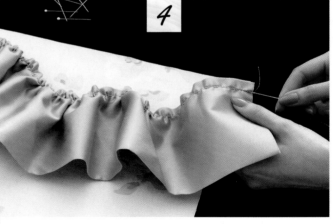

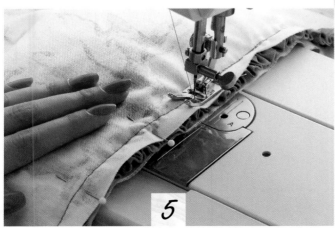

4 Divide ruffle strip and distance to be gathered on duvet cover front into fourths; pin-mark. Place ruffle strip on duvet cover front, right sides together, matching raw edges and pin marks; pull gathering cords to fit. Pin in place; stitch.

5 Pin front to back, right sides together. Stitch inside previous stitches. Turn right side out.

Making a
Duvet Cover with Welting

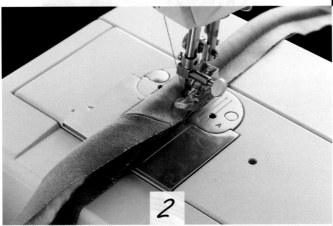

1 Follow steps 1 to 5 for basic duvet cover (page 18). Pin fabric around cording; measure this distance, and add 1" (2.5 cm) for seam allowances. Cut bias welting strips to this width, with combined length of strips equal to distance around duvet cover plus an allowance for seaming and easing.

2 Seam fabric strips together. Fold strip around cording, wrong sides together, matching raw edges. Using a zipper foot, machine-baste close to cording.

3 Stitch welting to right side of duvet front over previous stitches, matching raw edges and starting 2" (5 cm) from end of welting; clip and ease welting at corners, or ease at curves.

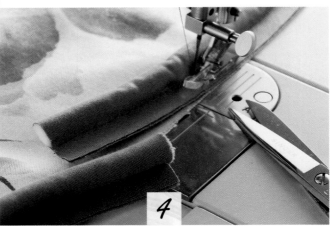

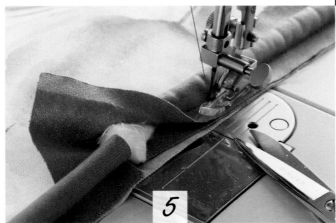

4 Stop stitching 2" (5 cm) from point where ends of welting will meet. Cut off one end of welting so it overlaps the other end by 1" (2.5 cm).

5 Remove stitching from one end of welting, and trim ends of cording so they just meet.

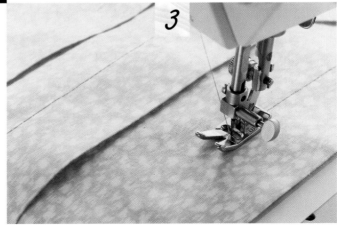

6 Fold under ½" (1.3 cm) of fabric on overlapping end; lap it around the other end. Finish stitching welting to duvet cover front. Pin duvet cover front to back, right sides together; stitch, crowding cording. Turn right side out.

Making a
Tucked Duvet Cover

1 Cut fabric for duvet cover front 19" (48.5 cm) wider and 1" (2.5 cm) longer than duvet. Use one full fabric width for center panel and two equal, partial widths for side panels. Two widths of fabric are needed for a twin-size or full-size duvet cover; three widths are needed for a queen-size or king-size cover. Cut fabric for back 1" (2.5 cm) wider than duvet and 1½" (3.8 cm) shorter than front. Cut a zipper strip 3½" (9 cm) wide and the same length as cut width of back.

2 Follow steps 2 to 5 on page 18. Wrong sides together, press foldline in center panel of pieced front, 2¾" (7 cm) from seamline. Press second foldline in center panel, 6" (15 cm) away from first foldline; press third foldline 6" (15 cm) away from second foldline. Repeat, pressing three foldlines on other side of center panel.

3 Stitch tucks 1½" (3.8 cm) from foldlines. For easier stitching, place tape on bed of sewing machine to use as a guide. Press tucks toward sides; outside tucks will cover seamlines. Complete as on page 18, step 6.

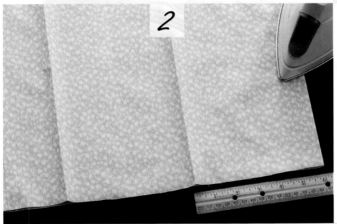

Bed SKIRTS

Bed skirts are used, in coordinated ensembles, with duvet covers, comforters, or quilts. They are designed to hide the box spring and legs of a bed. Choose from several styles, including gathered, tailored, and pleated.

For best results, attach the bed skirt to a fitted sheet to prevent the skirt from shifting out of position. Skirts for beds without footboards are sewn in one continuous strip around the sides and foot of the bed. When bed skirts are used on beds with footboards, the skirt is made in three sections and split at the corners.

To limit the number of seams in the skirt, the fabric is railroaded, which means that the lengthwise grain runs horizontally on the skirt. The design of the fabric is then turned sideways, so railroading is only suitable for solid colors or nondirectional prints. In most cases, three lengths can be cut from one width of 54" or 60" (137 or 152.5 cm) fabric. Railroading is essential for tailored skirts (page 26), which have long expanses of flat fabric between box pleats, and for pleated skirts (page 28). Gathered skirts (page 24) can be made from railroaded fabric or from multple widths cut on the crosswise grain.

MATERIALS

Decorator fabric; amount determined in worksheet for skirt style.

Fitted sheet.

Cord, such as pearl cotton, for the gathered bed skirt.

Tailored bed skirt (opposite) features deep 6" (15 cm) box pleats at each bottom corner and at the center of each side and 3" (7.5 cm) pleats at the head of the bed. This bed skirt has simple design lines and can be used for all styles of decorating, from traditional to contemporary.

Pleated bed skirt (near right) is a traditional style that works well for many room decors. The uniformly spaced pleats may be pressed in place for a crisp, tailored look or left unpressed for a softer look.

Gathered bed skirt (far right) adds a look of softness to the bedroom. Classic in style, it is suitable for many decorating schemes, including traditional and romantic country.

GATHERED BED SKIRT

WORKSHEET

Measure from line (step 1) to floor: Add 2" (5 cm)	+ 2"	
to find cut length of each piece.	=	
Measure the total length* of the marked line: Multiply by 2½	× 2½	
to find total width needed.	=	
Divide this number by the fabric width	÷	
to find number of pieces to cut.	=	
Multiply the number of pieces by the cut length	×	
to find total fabric length needed.	=	
If railroading, divide the total width by 3	÷ 3	
to find total fabric length needed.	=	

*To make a split-corner gathered bed skirt for a bed with a footboard, calculate the total width for each side and the foot separately.

Making a
Gathered Bed Skirt

1 Place fitted sheet over box spring. Using water-soluble marking pen or chalk, mark sheet along upper edge of box spring on each side and at foot of bed.

2 Stitch bed skirt pieces together. For a bed without a footboard, stitch pieces in one continuous strip; for a bed with a footboard, stitch pieces in three sections. Finish seam allowances by zigzagging or serging. Press and stitch 1" (2.5 cm) double-fold hems at sides and lower edge.

3 Zigzag over a cord on the right side at upper edge of skirt, within seam allowance, just beyond seamline. For more control when adjusting gathers, zigzag over second cord ¼" (6 mm) from first row.

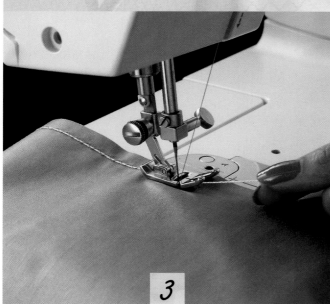

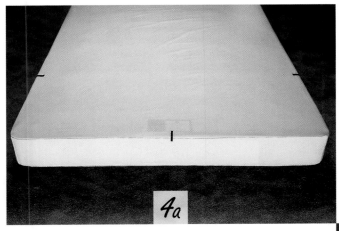

4a

(a) Bed without footboard. Divide upper edge of skirt and marked line on fitted sheet into fourths; mark.

(b) Bed with footboard. Mark corners at foot of bed. Divide upper edge of each skirt section in half; mark. Divide marked line on fitted sheet in half on each side and at foot of bed; mark.

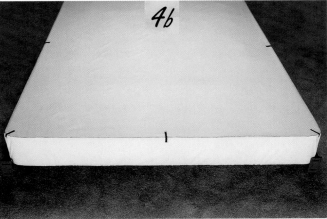

4b

5

5 Lay skirt right side down on top of box spring, matching marks; pin upper edge of skirt to sheet, extending 1/2" (1.3 cm) seam allowance beyond marked line. For split-corner skirt, butt hemmed edges together at corners.

6 Pull on gathering cords, and gather skirt evenly to fit. Pin in place.

7 Remove bed skirt and fitted sheet from the bed. Stitch the bed skirt to the fitted sheet, stitching 1/2" (1.3 cm) from raw edge; finish seam allowance.

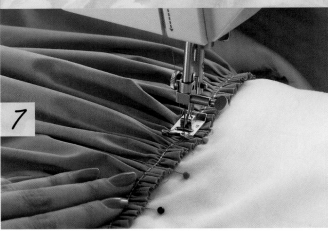

7

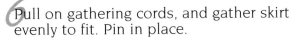

TAILORED BED SKIRT

Measure from line (step 1) to floor:

Add 2" (5 cm)   + 2

to find cut length of each piece.   =

One-piece skirt:
Measure the length of the box spring:

Add 23½" (59.8 cm)   + 23½"

to find total width needed for each side.   =

(Buy this amount of fabric that can be railroaded.)

Measure the foot of the box spring:
For twin or full, add 19" (48.5 cm)   + 19"

OR   OR

for queen or king*, add 31" (78.5 cm)   + 31"

to find total width needed for foot.   =

Split-corner skirt:
Measure the side of the box spring:

Add 28" (71 cm)   + 28"

to find total width needed for each side.   =

(Buy this amount of fabric that can be railroaded.)

Measure the foot of the box spring:
For twin or full, add 16" (40.5 cm)   + 16"

OR   OR

for queen or king*, add 28" (71 cm)   + 28"

to find total width needed for foot.   =

*Queen and king sizes have center pleat at foot.

2 Cut three lengthwise pieces from one fabric width, one for each side and one for foot of bed, with measurements determined in worksheet.

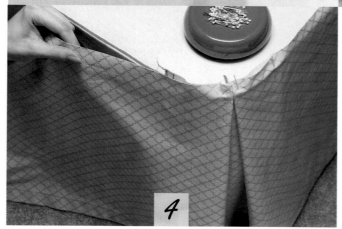

Making a
One-piece Tailored Bed Skirt

1 Place fitted sheet over box spring. Using water-soluble marking pen or chalk, mark sheet along upper edge of box spring on each side and at foot of bed. Mark corners at center of curve. Mark centers of side and foot sections.

3 Press and stitch 1" (2.5 cm) double-fold hems at lower edge and sides at head of bed. Stitch bed skirt pieces together; finish seam allowances.

4 Position bed skirt so the center of fabric is placed at center of foot. Fold pleats in place at markings as shown, with 3" (7.5 cm) on each side of pleat; pin to box spring with seam allowance extending above upper edge. Seams will be hidden in pleats.

5 Remove bed skirt from box spring, repositioning pins to secure pleats. Press pleats in place, with even pleat depth from upper edge to lower edge. Machine-baste ½" (1.3 cm) from upper edge, securing pleats.

6 Lay skirt right side down on top of the box spring. Pin the upper edge of bed skirt to the sheet, extending ½" (1.3 cm) seam allowance beyond marked line.

7 Remove bed skirt and fitted sheet from bed. Stitch bed skirt to sheet, stitching ½" (1.3 cm) from raw edge; finish seam allowance.

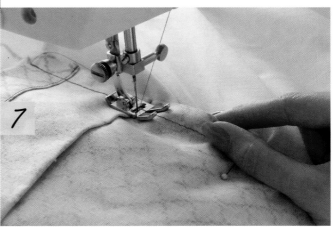

Making a
Split-corner Tailored Bed Skirt

1 Follow step 1, opposite. Cut three lengthwise pieces from one width of fabric, one piece for each side and one for the foot of the bed, with measurements determined in worksheet. Press and stitch 1" (2.5 cm) double-fold hems at lower edge and both sides of each piece.

2 Position each skirt section so center of fabric is placed at center of side or foot. Fold pleats in place at markings, with 3" (7.5 cm) on each side of pleat; pin to box spring with seam allowances extending above upper edge. Butt hemmed edges together at corners as shown. Finish bed skirt as in steps 5 to 7, above.

PLEATED BED SKIRT

Measure from line (step 1) to floor:
Add 2" (5 cm)   + 2"

to find cut length of each piece.   =

Measure the side of the box spring:
Multiply by 3   × 3

=

and add 12" (30.5 cm)   + 12"

to find total width needed for
each side.   =
(Buy this amount of fabric that can be
railroaded.)

Making a
One-piece Pleated Bed Skirt

1 Place fitted sheet over the box spring. Using water-soluble marking pen or chalk, mark sheet along the upper edge of box spring at each side and at foot of bed. Mark corners at center of curve. Divide and mark line at foot of bed for evenly spaced pleats, about 6" to 6½" (15 to 16.3 cm) apart. See guide. Repeat for each side.

NUMBER OF PLEATS

Bed size	Foot	Each side
Twin	6	12
Full	9	12
Queen	10	13
King	13	13

2 Cut three lengthwise pieces from one width of fabric, one piece for each side and one for the foot of the bed, with measurements determined in worksheet.

3 Press and stitch 1" (2.5 cm) double-fold hems at lower edges of bed skirt pieces. Position one bed skirt piece so center of fabric is placed at center of foot. Fold pleats in place from center of foot to corners, with depth on each side of pleat equal to one-half the distance between pleats; pin to box spring with seam allowance extending above upper edge.

4 Trim fabric 3½" (9 cm) beyond pleat foldline so seam will be concealed in pleat. Pin the side piece to the foot piece, pinning along ½" (1.3 cm) seam allowance. Pin pleats in place on side of bed. Repeat for other side.

5 Trim fabric 2" (5 cm) beyond the desired endpoint at head of bed. Pin 1" (2.5 cm) double-fold side hems in place.

6 Remove bed skirt from box spring, repositioning pins to secure pleats. Press pleats in place, if desired, with even pleat depth from upper edge to lower edge.

7 Stitch seams and side hems; finish the seam allowances. Machine-baste pleats in place 1/2" (1.3 cm) from upper edge.

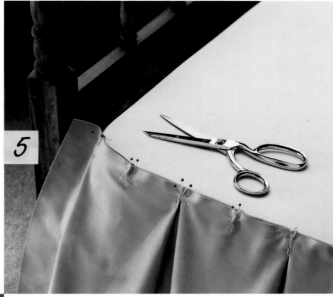

8 Lay bed skirt right side down on top of box spring. Pin upper edge of bed skirt to fitted sheet, extending 1/2" (1.3 cm) seam allowance beyond marked line.

9 Remove bed skirt and fitted sheet from bed. Stitch bed skirt to sheet, stitching 1/2" (1.3 cm) from raw edge; finish seam allowance.

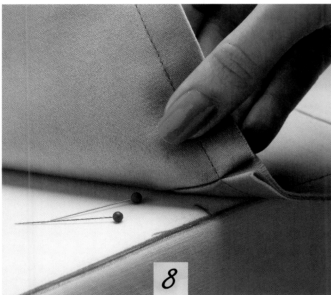

Making a
Split-corner Bed Skirt

1 Follow steps 1 to 3, opposite. At ends of foot section, trim fabric 2" (5 cm) beyond pleat foldline to allow for 1" (2.5 cm) double-fold side hem. Fold under 1" (2.5 cm) twice, and pin in place.

2 Pin side hem in place on the next bed skirt piece. Butt hemmed edges together at the corner; pin. Pin the pleats in place on side of bed. Repeat for other side. Follow steps 5 to 9, above.

Ideas for
BED SKIRTS

Make a simple bed skirt uniquely appealing by adding a border of fabric or lace to the lower edge of the skirt. Or combine the basic styles, making a double-layer bed skirt that consists of two skirts. For a double-layer bed skirt, make the underskirt, following the bed skirt instructions for the desired style (pages 24 to 29). Then make and attach a shorter bed skirt, with the seamline of the second skirt ½" (1.3 cm) above the previous seamline.

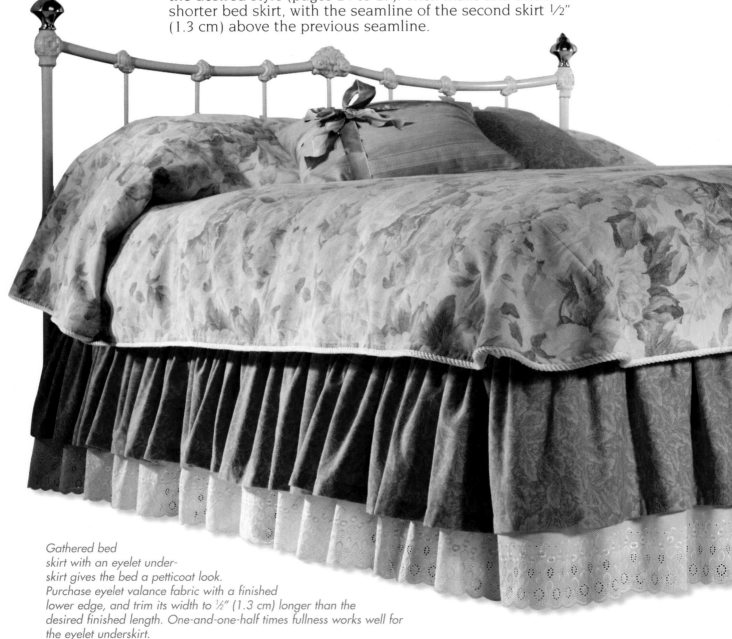

Gathered bed skirt with an eyelet under-skirt gives the bed a petticoat look. Purchase eyelet valance fabric with a finished lower edge, and trim its width to ½" (1.3 cm) longer than the desired finished length. One-and-one-half times fullness works well for the eyelet underskirt.

Bordered bed skirt (left) is made by piecing a fabric border at the lower edge. When cutting the fabric, allow for the extra seam allowances.

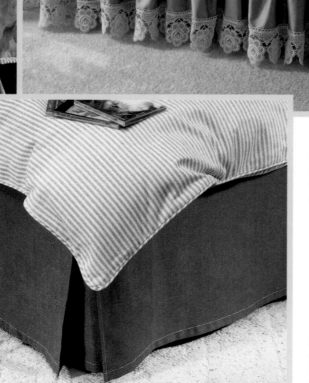

Lace-edged bed skirt (above) is made by applying a flat lace trim to the lower edge of the bed skirt, following the instructions for bedspreads (page 15).

Denim tailored bed skirt (left) gives a teenager's room a comfortable look. Topstitching accents the creases of the pleats and the lower hem.

Pillow SHAMS

For a coordinated bedroom set, sew pillow shams to match a duvet cover or bedspread. Pillow shams with flanges, welting, or ruffles are decorative covers for your bed pillows. These shams have simple lapped closures in the back, for easy insertion and removal of the pillows. A layer of polyester batting under the front gives the sham a slightly padded look. Machine quilting is used to outline designs in the fabric or create a dimensional image on solid colors.

Decorator fabric.

ite)
able
rom
po-
fin-
ge.

ght)
Large
central motif is quilted for a three-dimensional effect.

Decorative welting (bottom, right) is an elegant touch for simple motif-quilted shams.

FLANGED SHAMS

Pillow size	Cut size of front	Cut size of back piece A	Cut size of back piece B
Standard 20" × 26" (51 × 66 cm)	27" × 33" (68.5 × 84 cm)	27" × 24" (68.5 × 61 cm)	27" × 13" (68.5 × 33 cm)
Queen 20" × 30" (51 × 76 cm)	27" × 37" (68.5 × 94 cm)	27" × 28" (68.5 × 71 cm)	27" × 13" (68.5 × 33 cm)
King 20" × 36" (51 × 91.5 cm)	27" × 43" (68.5 × 109 cm)	27" × 34" (68.5 × 86.5 cm)	27" × 13" (68.5 × 33 cm)

Making a
Flanged Sham

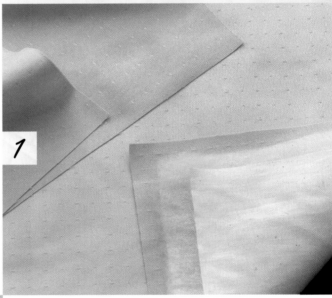

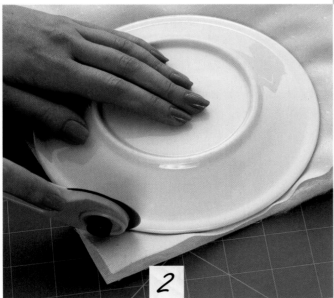

1 Cut pieces for the sham as indicated in the guide. Also cut one batting piece and one lining piece the same size as the front.

2 Mark quilting design on sham front, if necessary. Plan for 3" (7.5 cm) flange and $1/2$" (1.3 cm) seam allowance. Layer sham front over batting and lining; baste together, using safety pins. Mark rounded corners, using a saucer; trim.

3 Machine-quilt on marked lines, using an Even Feed® foot. Or, for fabric with large central motif, quilt on design lines in motif. Baste layers together ¼" (6 mm) from outer edge.

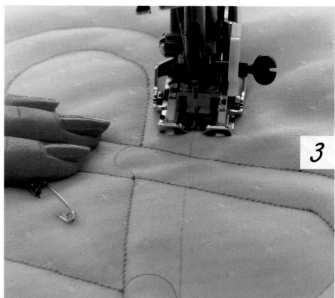

4 Make and apply fabric-covered welting, if desired, to sham front as on page 20, steps 1 to 6. Or, apply twisted welting as on page 38, steps 1 to 6.

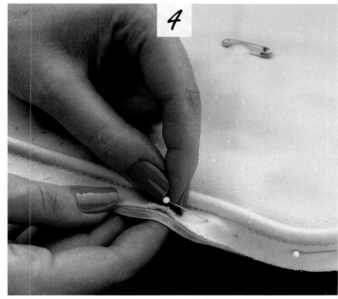

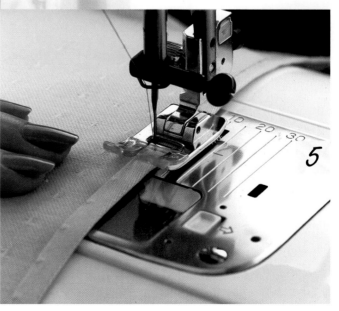

5 Turn under ¼" (6 mm) on overlap end of back piece A; press. Turn under and press again, forming ¼" (6 mm) double hem. Stitch just inside inner fold. Repeat for overlap side of back piece B.

Continued

6 Lap piece B over piece A 3″ (7.5 cm). Sham back should be the same length as sham front. Hand-baste lapped pieces together across back.

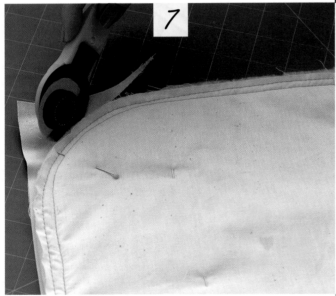

7 Place sham front over sham back, right sides together. Trim corners of back to match front. Pin front to back; stitch ½″ (1.3 cm) seam, crowding welting, if used. Remove basting thread at overlap; turn sham right side out through opening. Steam outer edge as necessary.

8 Mark stitching line for flange on sham front 3″ (7.5 cm) from welted seams, using removable tape; mark rounded corners with chalk, using water glass as guide. Pin layers together near stitching line. Topstitch along edge of tape; remove tape.

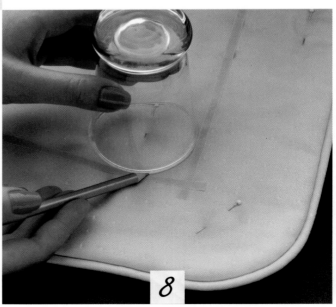

RUFFLED OR WELTED SHAMS

	Pillow size	Cut size of front	Cut size of back piece A	Cut size of back piece B
G U I D E	Standard 20" × 26" (51 × 66 cm)	21" × 27" (53.5 × 68.5 cm)	21" × 21" (53 × 53 cm)	21" × 10" (53 × 25.5 cm)
	Queen 20" × 30" (51 × 76 cm)	21" × 31" (53.5 × 78.5 cm)	21" × 23" (53 × 58.5 cm)	21" × 10" (53 × 25.5 cm)
	King 20" × 36" (51 × 91.5 cm)	21" × 37" (53.5 × 94 cm)	21" × 29" (53 × 73.5 cm)	21" × 10" (53 × 25.5 cm)

Making a
Ruffled Sham

1 Cut pieces for the sham as indicated in the guide. Also cut one batting piece and one lining piece the same size as the front. Cut fabric strips for ruffle on crosswise or lengthwise grain, with combined length of strips two times circumference of sham; width of strips is two times the finished width of ruffle plus 1" (2.5 cm) for seam allowances. Follow steps 2 and 3, pages 34 and 35, omitting reference to flange.

2 Stitch fabric strips for ruffle together in 1/4" (6 mm) seams, right sides together. Stitch ends of ruffle strip together, forming a continuous strip. Fold pieced strip in half lengthwise, wrong sides together; press.

3 Follow steps 3 to 4 for duvet cover with ruffle (page 19), distributing gathers evenly on all four sides of sham. Finish as on pages 35 and 36, steps 5 to 7.

Making a
Sham with Twisted Welting

*If you select twisted welting that twists in the opposite direction from the welting shown, interchange the use of the words "left" and "right" in steps 3 to 5.

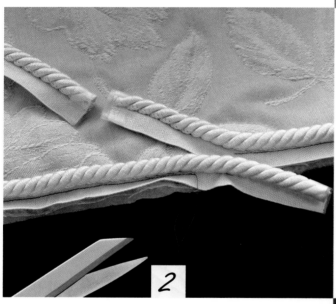

1 Follow steps 1 to 3 on page 34, omitting reference to flange. Identify right side of twisted welting; from right side, inner edge of tape is not visible. Baste twisted welting to sham front, right sides up, with cord along ½" (1.3 cm) seamline, using zipper foot; leave 3" (7.5 cm) tail at beginning. Wrap transparent tape around end of tail to prevent raveling.

2 Leave 1" (2.5 cm) unstitched between ends. Cut welting, leaving 3" (7.5 cm) tail; wrap end with tape.

3 Remove stitching from welting tape on tails. Trim welting tape to 1" (2.5 cm) from stitching; overlap ends, and secure with tape. Arrange twisted cording with the cording at left turned up and the cording at right turned down.

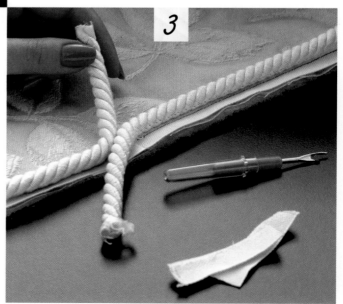

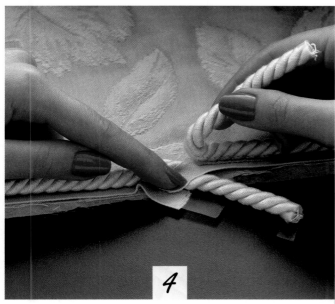

4 Insert cording at left under the welting tape, untwisting and flattening it under the welting tape as shown. Tape in place.

5 Place cording at right over cording at left until lapped area looks like continuous twisted welting; manipulate the cording as necessary, untwisting it partially to flatten it at seamline. Tape in place. Check the appearance on both sides of tape.

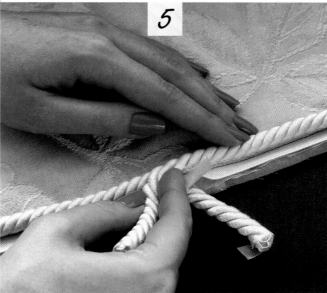

6 Machine-baste through all layers to secure welting at seamline; use zipper foot, positioned so you can stitch in the direction of the twists.

7 Finish seam allowances. Finish sham as on pages 35 and 36, steps 5 to 7.

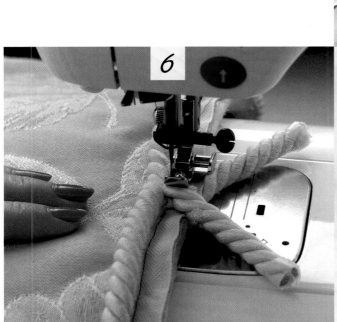

Decorative Closures for SHAMS & DUVETS

Decorative closures give duvet covers and shams distinctive style. Select from several closure methods, including a basic lapped button closure, welted closures, and banded closures with buttons or with grommets and ties. The basic button closure can be sewn either vertically at the center or horizontally, depending on the look you prefer. Banded or welted closures work best horizontally. A horizontal closure on a duvet cover should be positioned so that it will not be covered by shams and other pillows at the head of the bed.

Use the worksheets to determine the fabric needs and sizes to cut the front pieces. If you are using a patterned fabric that should be matched at the closure, it may be helpful to develop a paper pattern to help you determine where to cut the pieces. Also remember to purchase extra fabric to allow for matching the pattern (page 125).

Select buttons that will make a statement, preferably at least 1" (2.5 cm) in diameter. Smaller buttons may be dwarfed in relation to the entire bedding ensemble. For a coordinated set, repeat the closure treatment used for the duvet cover in the pillow shams.

MATERIALS

Fabric, amount determined in worksheet.

Contrasting fabric, for banded closure and ties.

Cording and contrasting fabric for welted closure.

Buttons; decorative or fabric-covered at least 1" (2.5 cm) in diameter.

⅜" (1 cm) grommets and attaching tool, for grommet closure.

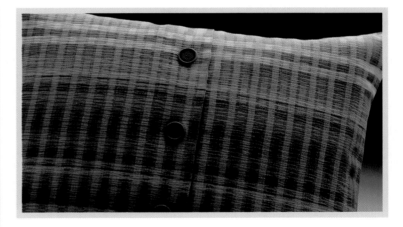

Animal-print banding with grommets and ties (opposite) creates exotic style for this bedroom ensemble.

Vertical lapped closure (top, right) gives the look of a classic plaid shirt. Horizontal welted closure with fabric-covered buttons (bottom, right) is an elegant tailored look. Note how the patterns are matched for both closure styles.

Sewing a
Vertical Lapped Closure

VERTICAL LAPPED CLOSURE

W O R K S H E E T

VERTICAL LAPPED CLOSURE

Measure the length (vertically)
of the duvet or pillow:

Add 1" (2.5 cm)   + 1"

to find cut length for front.   =

Measure the width (horizontally)
of the duvet or pillow:

Add 10" (25.5 cm)   + 10"

to find width needed for front.   =

Divide by 2   ÷ 2

to find cut width of each front side.   =

1 Cut fabric for duvet cover or sham back 1" (2.5 cm) wider and longer than the duvet or pillow. If piecing is necessary, use one full fabric width for center panel and two equal, partial widths for side panels.

2 Cut two pieces for front, with measurements as determined in worksheet. Finish inner edges of front pieces, using serger or multistitch-zigzag; press under 3" (7.5 cm). Blindstitch or topstitch facing in place, if desired.

3 Mark top and bottom buttonholes no more than 8" (20.5 cm) from ends and 1½" (3.8 cm) from pressed fold; space remaining buttonholes evenly. Stitch buttonholes parallel to fold.

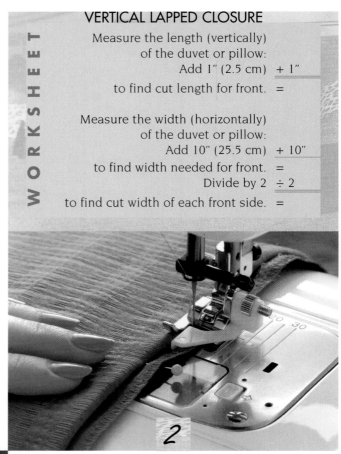

4 Overlap front pieces 3" (7.5 cm); secure with safety pins, inserting from wrong side. Baste overlaps ⅜" (1 cm) from ends.

5 Pin front to back, right sides together; stitch ½" (1.3 cm) seam. Remove several safety pins; turn right side out through opening. Press. Mark placement for buttons; sew in place.

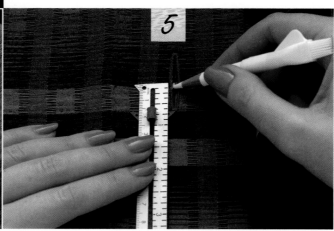

Sewing a
Horizontal Lapped Closure

1 Follow steps 1 and 2, opposite, using horizontal lapped closure worksheet. Mark end buttonholes no more than 8" (20.5 cm) from sides and 1½" (3.8 cm) from pressed fold on upper section; space remaining buttonholes evenly. Stitch buttonholes parallel to fold. Finish as in steps 4 and 5, opposite.

HORIZONTAL LAPPED CLOSURE

WORKSHEET

Determine finished length of duvet or sham from top to center of closure:

Add 5" (12.5 cm)   + 5" _____

to find cut length of top piece.   = _____

Determine finished length of duvet or sham from center of closure to bottom:

Add 5" (12.5 cm)   + 5" _____

to find cut length of bottom piece.   = _____

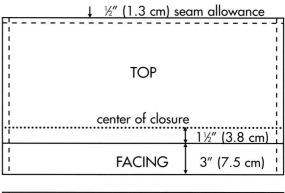

½" (1.3 cm) seam allowance

TOP

center of closure

1½" (3.8 cm)

FACING   3" (7.5 cm)

FACING   3" (7.5 cm)

1½" (3.8 cm)

center of closure

BOTTOM

½" (1.3 cm) seam allowance

Sewing a
Welted Lapped Closure

1 Follow step 1, opposite. Cut fabric for front with length as determined in worksheet, below; cut width equals pillow or duvet width plus 1" (2.5 cm). Also cut 3½" (9 cm) facing strip with length equal to cut width of front. Finish upper edge of bottom front piece; press under 3" (7.5 cm). Finish one long edge of facing.

WELTED LAPPED CLOSURE

WORKSHEET

Determine finished length of duvet or sham from top to center of closure:

Add 2½" (6.5 cm)   + 2½" _____

to find cut length of top piece.   = _____

Determine finished length of duvet or sham from center of closure to bottom:

Add 5" (12.5 cm)   + 5" _____

to find cut length of bottom piece.   = _____

½" (1.3 cm) seam allowance

TOP

center of closure

1½" (3.8 cm)

½" (1.3 cm) seam allowance

FACING STRIP   3½" (9 cm)

FACING   3" (7.5 cm)

1½" (3.8 cm)

center of closure

BOTTOM

½" (1.3 cm) seam allowance

Continued

Sewing a
Welted Lapped Closure
(continued)

2 Cut bias strips and prepare welting, page 20, steps 1 and 2; prepare enough to welt overlap and outer edges of cover or sham. Apply welting to lower edge of top front. Trim cord out of welting ½" (1.3 cm) from each end.

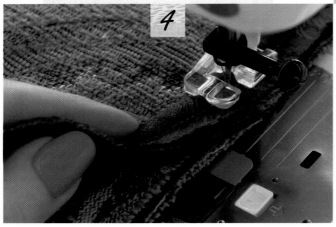

3 Pin unfinished edge of facing over welted edge, right sides together; stitch, crowding cording. Turn facing to inside, and press.

4 Apply welting to outer edge of front, pages 20 and 21, steps 3 to 6. Finish as on page 42, steps 4 and 5.

Sewing a
Banded Closure

1 Follow step 1, page 42. Cut fabric for front with length as determined in worksheet; cut width equals pillow or duvet width plus 1" (2.5 cm). Also cut 9" (23 cm) banding strip with length equal to cut width of front. Finish upper edge of bottom front; press under 4" (10 cm). Secure facing in place, if desired.

BANDED CLOSURE

WORKSHEET

Determine finished length of duvet or sham from top to center of closure:

Subtract 1" (2.5 cm) – 1"

to find cut length of top piece. =

Determine finished length of duvet or sham from center of closure to bottom:

Add 6½" (16.3 cm) + 6½"

to find cut length of bottom piece. =

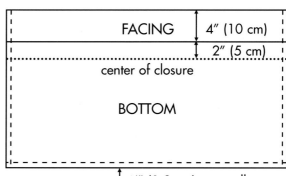

½" (1.3 cm) seam allowance

TOP

center of closure

2" (5 cm)

½" (1.3 cm) seam allowance

BAND   9" (23 cm)

FACING   4" (10 cm)

2" (5 cm)

center of closure

BOTTOM

½" (1.3 cm) seam allowance

2 Press banding in half lengthwise; unfold. Finish one long edge, using serger or multistitch-zigzag. Pin opposite edge to lower edge of top piece, right sides together; stitch ½" (1.3 cm) seam.

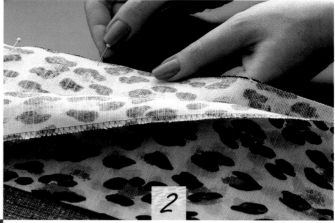

3 Press seam allowances toward banding. Refold banding on center foldline, folding finished edge to back over seam; pin. Topstitch ¼" (6 mm) from edge of banding, catching finished edge in stitching. Mark and stitch buttonholes, evenly spaced, along center of band. Finish as on page 42, steps 4 and 5.

Making a
Grommet and Tie Closure

1 Sew duvet cover or sham as in steps 1 to 3, opposite and above, but install grommets at center of band. Cut 2" × 16" (5 × 40.5 cm) bias strips for ties, one for each grommet. Press ends under ¼" (6 mm). Press strip in half lengthwise, wrong sides together. Turn raw edges in to center fold; press. Refold strip, and pin. Edgestitch ends and along folds. Repeat for all strips.

2 Center a tie under each grommet; stitch securely. Insert pillow or duvet. To close, insert ties through grommets, and tie in knots or bows.

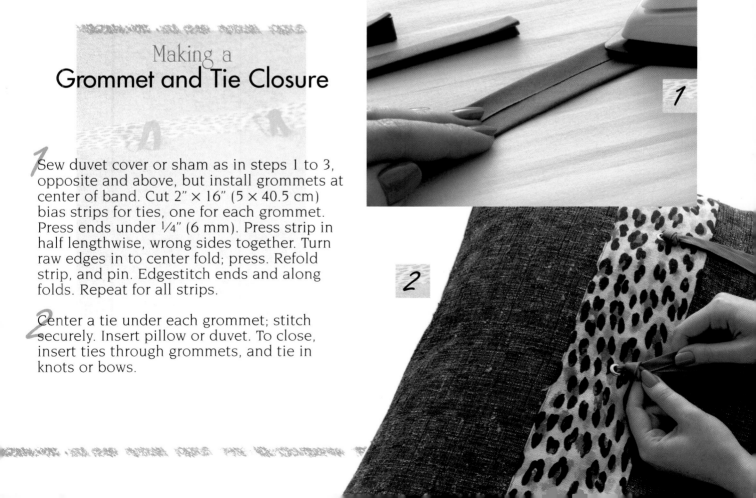

Decorative Details for
BED LINENS

Designer bed linens with decorative detailing can be pretty costly, but you can design and create your own, using plain sheets and pillowcases that are far more affordable. Coordinate decorative detailing on bed linens with the bedspread or duvet cover and shams you have made, for a completely coordinated ensemble.

If you have a sewing machine that is capable of stitching embroidered designs, bed linens are a great place to use them. Follow your sewing machine owner's manual to embroider simple repeating designs or more elaborate motifs and monograms on the existing hems of pillowcases and flat sheets. Sew appliqués (page 114) using fabric scraps from other elements of the ensemble, even repeating the appliqué used on bath towels. Or, replace plain hems with coordinating fabric borders.

MATERIALS

Washable fabrics and trims.

Machine embroidery thread.

Tear-away stabilizer.

Fabric border with contrast flat piping (opposite) coordinates sheets and pillowcases with the duvet cover and bed skirt for a designer look.

Machine-embroidered motifs (below) give ordinary bed linens distinctive taste.

Sewing
Contrasting Borders on Bed Linens

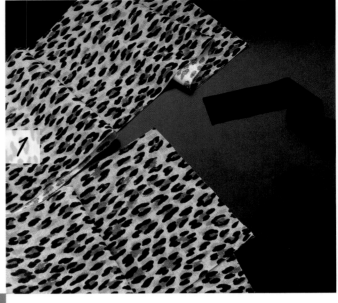

1. Prewash fabric and any trim. Cut border fabric to necessary length plus 1" (2.5 cm) for seam allowances; width should equal twice the desired finished border depth plus 1" (2.5 cm) for seam allowances. Cut 2" (5 cm) strip for flat piping, if desired, to same length as border fabric. Cut fabric and prepare corded welting (page 20), if desired. Seam pieces together as necessary.

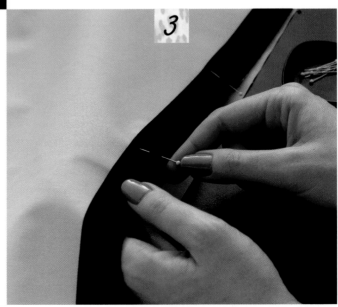

2. Trim off existing hem from pillowcase or sheet. For pillowcase, remove stitches to open side seam about 4" (10 cm). Omit step 3 if flat piping or corded welting is not desired.

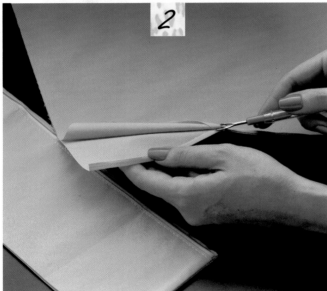

3. Press ends of flat piping strip under ½" (1.3 cm), if sewing to sheet. Press strip in half lengthwise, wrong sides together. Pin to right side of sheet or pillowcase, aligning raw edges; stitch ½" (1.3 cm) seam. Or, stitch corded welting to right side of upper edge, with stitching line ½" (1.3 cm) from edge; press under ends ½" (1.3 cm), if sewing to sheet.

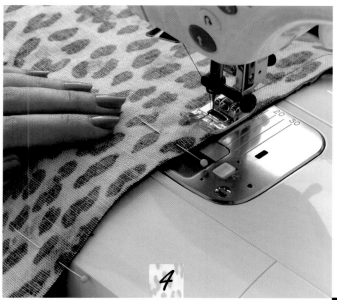

4 Press under ½" (1.3 cm) on one long edge of border. Pin other edge, right side down, to wrong side of sheet or pillowcase. Stitch ½" (1.3 cm) seam.

5 Press seam allowances toward border. For sheet, press ends under even with side hems of sheet; trim seam allowance to ½" (1.3 cm), if necessary. Wrap border to right side, just covering stitching line with folded edge. Press and pin.

6 Topstitch close to fold; for sheet, also top-stitch ends closed. Use zipper foot if sewing next to corded welting.

7 Stitch pillowcase side seam and border closed. Trim border seam allowances; finish, using serger or zigzag stitch.

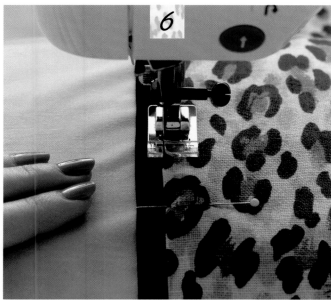

Machine
Embroidery Tips

Planning pattern placement for hooped designs. Make practice pattern as template; mark horizontal and vertical guidelines on template. Transfer guidelines to sheet or pillowcase hem, using water-soluble marker.

Stabilizing. Place one or more layers of tear-away stabilizer or water-soluble stabilizer under fabric, to prevent puckering. Densely embroidered designs tend to pucker more, requiring firm stabilizer.

Hooped designs. Baste similar-weight fabric to hem edge before inserting into hoop, if necessary, so that hem can be held taut in all directions. Remove after stitching is complete.

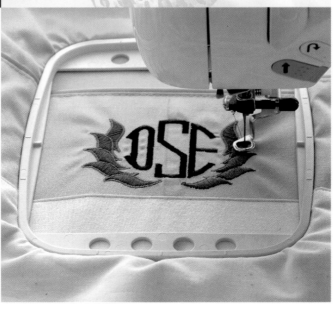

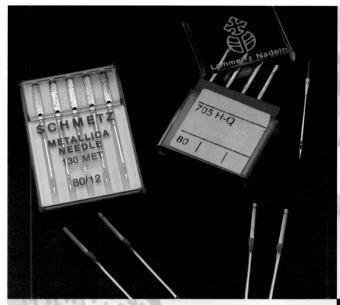

Needles. Insert new sharp needle with each project. Specialty needles, such as the Metalfil® needle by Lamertz, are helpful for some threads. The longer eye is easier to thread, and the fine point makes smaller holes.

Thread. Use fine cotton or polyester machine embroidery bobbin thread for minimal bulk. Wind the bobbin slowly to help prevent puckering. There are a variety of machine embroidery threads available, including cotton, rayon, and metallic threads. They produce durable embroidered stitches with a soft sheen.

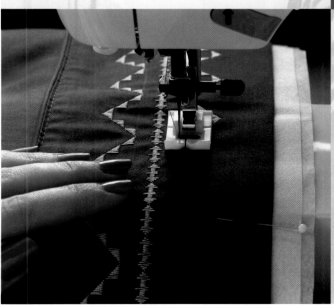

Straight-line patterns. Mark a guideline parallel to the hem edge, using water-soluble marker. Guide presser foot parallel to marked line for accuracy.

Bedside CADDY

You'll never have to hunt for the remote control, your reading glasses, or your favorite book. Keep them all neatly at hand in this bedside caddy.

Make the caddy from fabric to match or coordinate with the bed skirt or duvet cover. The caddy features one deep pocket, about 11½" (29.3 cm) wide, perfect for holding your current novel, and four pockets 5¾" (14.5 cm) wide for any other bedside amenities. A fabric extension slips between the mattress and box spring to hold the caddy securely in place.

Tailored bedside caddy (opposite) has narrow contrast piping accenting the front pocket.

Eyelet trim adds a feminine touch to the caddy at right.

Making a
Bedside Caddy

FRONT 13" × 13" (33 × 33 cm)	BACKING 13" × 13" (33 × 33 cm)	FRONT POCKET 13" × 7¾" (33 × 20 cm)
		MIDDLE POCKET 13" × 9" (33 × 23 cm)
EXTENSION 23" × 10" (58.5 × 25.5 cm)	BIAS BINDING 2½" × 64" (6.5 × 163 cm)	BACK POCKET 13" × 9½" (33 × 24.3 cm)

1 Cut pieces for the caddy as shown in the diagram at left. Also cut a 13" (33 cm) square of polyester fleece and a contrasting bias strip for piping.

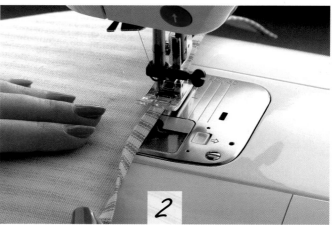

2 Press under ¼" (6 mm) twice at top of back pocket. Stitch close to fold, forming double hem. Repeat for middle pocket.

3 Prepare piping as for welting, page 20, steps 1 and 2, if desired. Baste piping or lace edging to top of front pocket, with stitching line scant ¼" (6 mm) below upper edge.

4 Cut 13" (33 cm) bias strip for binding; fold in half lengthwise, and press, taking care not to distort the strip width. Pin strip to upper edge of front pocket, aligning raw edges. Stitch ¼" (6 mm) from edge, crowding piping, if used.

5 Wrap binding strip snugly over pocket edge, covering stitching line on pocket back; pin in the ditch of the seam. Stitch in the ditch on right side of pocket, catching binding on back of pocket.

6 Layer three pocket pieces, aligning lower and side edges; upper edges should be ½" (1.3 cm) apart. Stitch from top to bottom through center of pockets.

7 Layer pockets over caddy front, right sides up. Align all sides and lower edges; pin. Mark seamline around outer edge, forming 12" (30.5 cm) square. Round off the last 2" (5 cm) at each corner.

8 Fold extension crosswise, right sides together. Sew ½" (1.3 cm) seams on long sides. Trim corners; turn right side out, and press.

9 Place backing on work surface; cover with fleece. Place caddy front over fleece, aligning edges. Pin raw edges of extension to upper edge of caddy back, matching centers. Baste all pieces together, stitching just outside the marked line. Trim excess fabric and fleece to scant ¼" (6 mm) beyond marked line.

10 Seam bias strips as necessary. Cut end at 45° angle; press under ½" (1.3 cm). Fold strip in half lengthwise, and press.

11 Stitch binding to right side of caddy, aligning raw edges, and beginning with folded end at one side. Stitch ¼" (6 mm) from edge. Trim opposite end at 45° angle to lap over folded end by ⅜" (1 cm). Finish binding as in step 5, opposite.

Sheer Overlay PILLOWS

Knife-edge pillows encased in sheer flanged overlays have a dreamy, dainty look, perfect for a feminine bedroom. For the inner pillow, select solid-color fabrics in pure medium tones. The sheer white overlay lightens the color to pastel and creates the look of a frosty window. Embellishments on the surface of the knife-edge pillow, such as monograms, doilies, or silk flowers, take on a subtle shadowy appearance. Or, the overlay itself can be decorated with ribbons, double-needle stitching, or shadow appliqués made from sheer fusible interfacing.

MATERIALS

Lightweight fabric for inner knife-edge pillow, such as broadcloth or batiste.

Sheer white fabric for overlay, such as organdy, dotted Swiss, or lawn.

Embellishments for inner pillow, such as doilies, narrow trims and ribbons, and silk flowers.

Sheer fusible interfacing, for shadow appliqués.

Pillow form in desired size, or polyester fiberfill.

Making a
Knife-edge Pillow

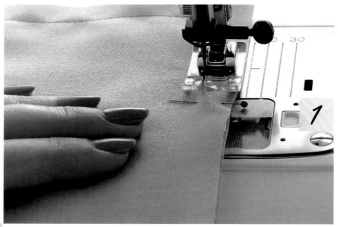

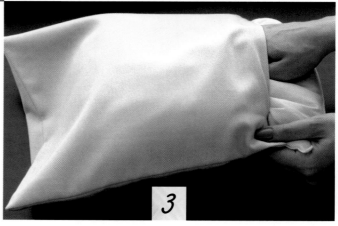

1 Cut front and back 1" (2.5 cm) wider and longer than the desired finished size. Embellish as desired (page 60). Pin the pieces right sides together; stitch ½" (1.3 cm) seam, leaving an opening on one side for turning and stuffing.

2 Trim corners diagonally, ⅛" (3 mm) from stitching. Turn pillow right side out, pulling out corners. Press seams. Also, press under the seam allowances in the opening.

3 Insert pillow form, or stuff pillow with polyester fiberfill, gently pulling pieces apart to fluff and separate fibers. Work filling into corners, using long, blunt tool, such as a wooden spoon handle.

4 Pin opening closed; slipstitch.

Making a
Sheer Flanged Overlay

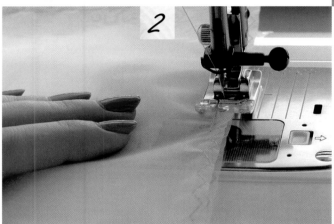

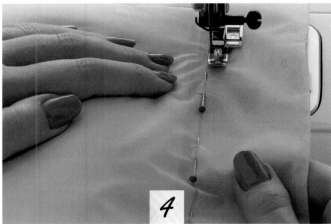

1 Cut front and back 5½" (14 cm) wider and longer than the inner pillow. Embellish as desired (page 61). Pin the pieces right sides together; stitch ½" (1.3 cm) seam, leaving an opening on one side for turning and inserting inner pillow.

2 Trim corners diagonally, ⅛" (3 mm) from stitching. Trim seams to ¼" (6 mm); finish the seam allowances together, to prevent fraying; finish the seam allowances in opening separately.

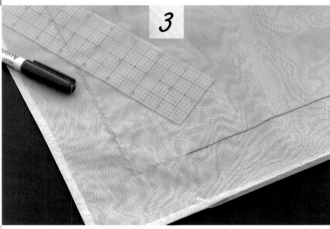

3 Turn overlay right side out; press. Also, press under the seam allowances in the opening. Mark a line 2" (5 cm) from outer edge. Topstitch on marked line, beginning and ending at opening.

4 Insert inner pillow. Finish topstitching. Slipstitch outer opening closed.

Techniques for
Sheer Overlay Pillows

Doily. Sew a doily or vintage handkerchief onto the front of the inner pillow.

Silk flowers. Remove silk flower petals and leaves from stems. Plan flower placement on pillow front. Secure with small hand stitches. Stitch small pearl at each flower center, if desired.

Decorative cording. Transfer design to typing paper; pin to right side of pillow front. Straight-stitch through center of narrow braid, following design lines, backstitching at beginning and end. Apply liquid fray preventer to ends; allow to dry. Tear away paper.

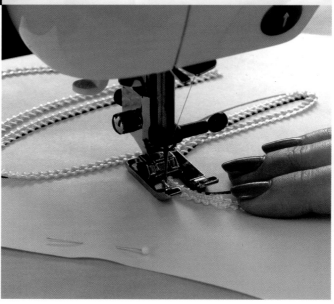

Shadow appliqués. Cut desired shapes from sheer fusible knit interfacing. Fuse to wrong side of overlay front. Protect ironing board with press cloth or paper. Straight-stitch design lines over appliqués from right side, if desired.

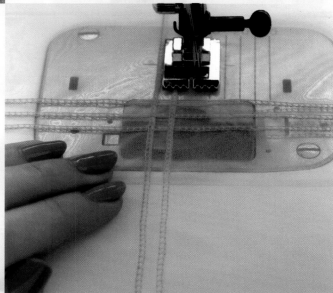

Twin-needle stitching. Stitch rows of pintucks on right side of overlay front, using twin needle and pintuck foot. Grooves on bottom of pintuck foot ride over previous ridges, allowing you to sew multiple parallel rows of pintucks.

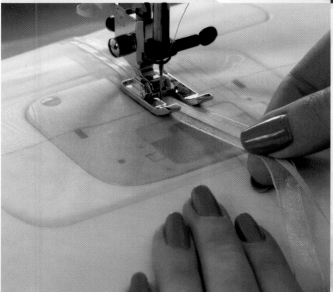

Ribbons. Stitch narrow ribbons to right side of overlay front. Plan placement to frame inner pillow embellishments, if desired. Catch ribbon ends in outer seams of overlay flange.

Rod-pocket CURTAINS

Rod-pocket curtains and valances are a simple and versatile treatment for windows or tub openings. The look can be varied by the fabric choice, the choice of the curtain rod, the length of the treatment, and how the fabric is draped. You may use a 1", 2", or 4½" (2.5, 6.5, or 11.5 cm) curtain rod or a drapery pole set, depending on the look you prefer.

The basic construction steps of all rod-pocket styles are the same. Essentially, rod-pocket treatments are flat panels of fabric with stitched-in headings, rod pockets, and double-fold hems. Two curtain panels can be separated in the center and drawn to the sides. One panel drawn to a side works well for very narrow windows. Some unique looks can be achieved by styling the curtains or valances in interesting ways, as shown opposite.

Before you sew, install the curtain rod or pole (page 75). Measure from the bottom of the rod to where you want the lower edge of the treatment. To determine the finished length of the curtain, add the desired heading depth and the depth of the rod pocket to this measurement. This is what the curtain will measure from the top of the heading to the lower edge.

The cut width of the curtain is determined by the width of the window and the amount of fullness desired in the curtain. For sheer fabrics, allow two-and-one-half to three times the width of the window for fullness; for heavier fabrics, allow for two to two-and-one-half times fullness.

MATERIALS

Decorator fabric, amount determined in worksheet.

Curtain rod or pole set.

Separate center panels (opposite) are swagged across the side panels and looped over the decorative rod between the finial and the outer edge, forming casual casades. This style works best with lightweight fabrics or sheers.

Valance and cafe curtains (left) have casual style. On a double-hung window, mount the lower curtain rod above the center of the window.

Colorful tieback curtains (right) perk up a small window.

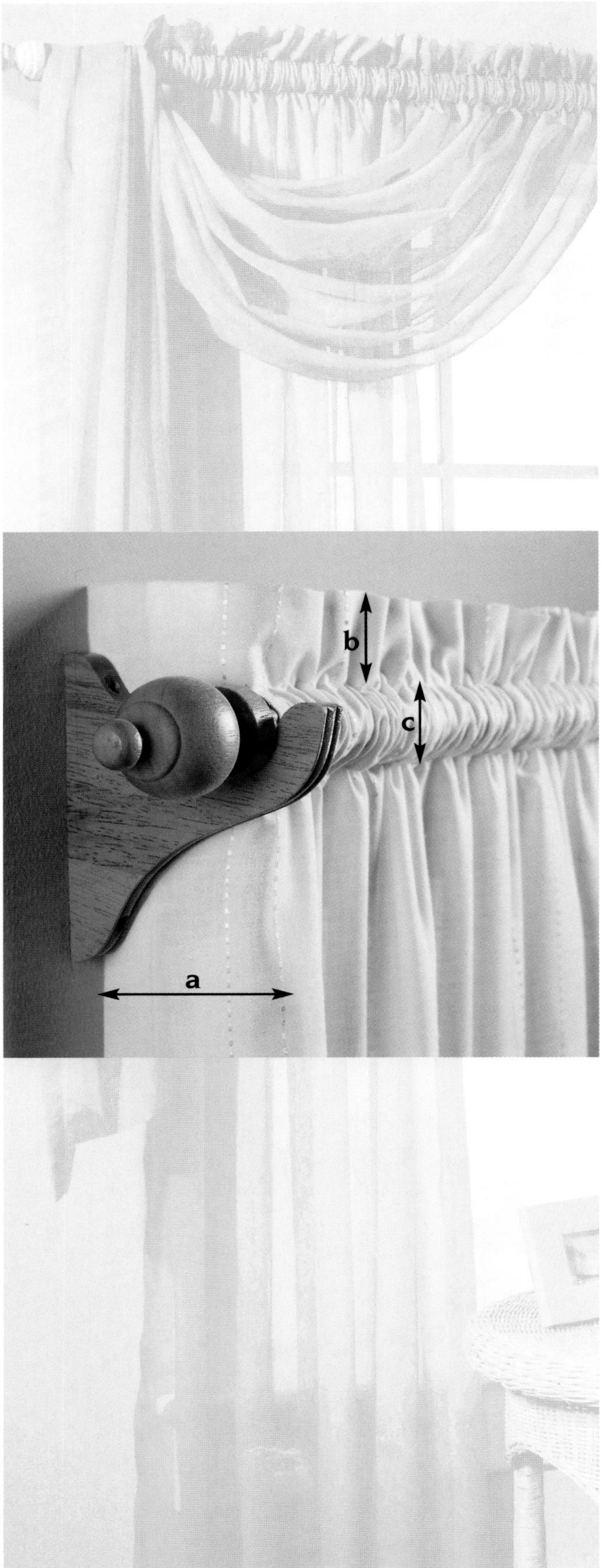

TERMS TO KNOW

The return (**a**) is the portion of the treatment extending from the end of the rod to the wall, blocking the side light and view. The heading (**b**) is the portion at the top of the treatment that forms a ruffle above the rod. The depth of the heading is the distance from the top of the finished curtain to the top stitching line of the rod pocket. The rod pocket (**c**) is the portion of the treatment, between two stitching lines, where the rod or pole is inserted. To determine the depth of the rod pocket, measure around the widest point of the rod or pole; add 1/2" (1.3 cm) for ease, and divide this amount by two.

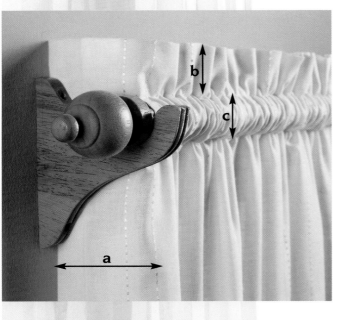

ROD-POCKET CURTAINS

WORKSHEET

Measure the desired finished length:	
Add the hem allowance (below).	+
Add 1/2" (1.3 cm) for turn-under at top.	+ 1/2"
Add the rod-pocket depth.	+
Add the heading depth	+
to find cut length of each piece.	=
Measure rod length with returns:	
Multiply by the desired fullness	×
to find cut width (after piecing).	=
Divide by the fabric width	÷
(round up to nearest whole number*)	
to find number of widths needed.	=
Multiply by the cut length	×
to find total amount of fabric needed.	=

*Use only full and half widths of fabric in each panel. Rounding up will add slightly more fullness.

HEM ALLOWANCES

GUIDE

Valances:	4" (10 cm)
Sill-length:	6" (15 cm)
Floor-length:	8" (20.5 cm)
Shower curtains:	6" (15 cm)

*All hems are double-folded.

Making a
Rod-pocket Curtain

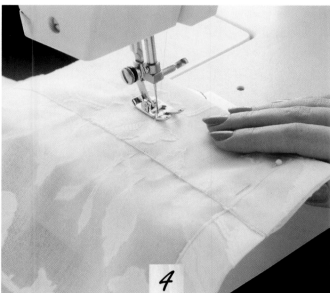

1. Seam fabric widths, if necessary, for each curtain panel. Stitch French seams, if desired, or finish both seam allowances together, and press to one side. At lower edge, press under the hem allowance twice to wrong side; stitch to make double-fold hem.

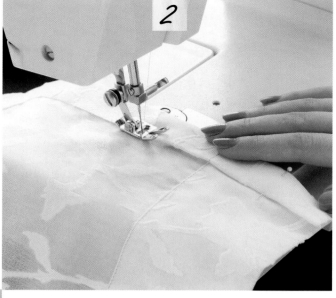

2. Press under 1" (2.5 cm) twice on sides. Stitch to make double-fold side hems.

3. Press under ½" (1.3 cm) on upper edge. Then press under an amount equal to rod-pocket depth plus heading depth.

4. Stitch close to first fold. Mark heading depth; stitch again at marked depth. As a guide for easier stitching, apply masking tape to sewing machine bed.

5. Insert curtain rod through rod pocket, gathering fabric evenly. Install rod on brackets.

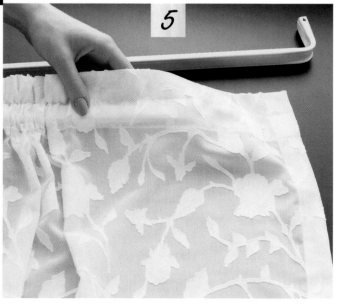

Ideas for ROD-POCKET CURTAINS

Rod-pocket curtains are very versatile. Variety in styling is achieved by varying the heading depth, the fullness, and the manner in which the curtain is mounted and dressed. They also work to filter the light entering the room or provide a degree of privacy. Color, texture, and creative embellishments reinforce the total design concept of the bedroom or bathroom.

Softly gathered valance falling from the curtain top (above) is really a 16" (40.5 cm) heading. After pressing and pinning the heading in place, roll it down, to minimize bulk as you sew the rod pocket. For best results, mount the curtains on a 2½" (6.5 cm) flat rod.

Two-tone curtain (top, right) serves double duty. The sheer top allows light to enter the room, while the opaque bottom preserves your privacy. Before hemming the sides, seam the top and bottom, wrong sides together, and cover the seam allowances with a decorative trim or bias fabric band (page 117).

Diaphanous sheers (opposite and right) filter the sunlight from a bathroom window. Mounted on simple curtain rods, the 8" (20.5 cm) heading droops forward in a lazy flounce. Shadowy figures are simple fusible interfacing appliqués (page 61). Many techniques used on sheer overlay pillows (page 57) can also be used on sheer curtains.

Curtain TIEBACKS

Many rod-pocket curtains are drawn back and held in place with tiebacks. Tiebacks offer a decorative opportunity to repeat a design or embellishment used elsewhere in the room. For example, the shirred effect created by a rod pocket can be repeated in a shirred tieback. You may want to sew fabric bands, narrow trims, or galloon lace onto tiebacks with tucked ends, to coordinate with decorative towels (page 111) or shower curtains (pages 96 and 97). These tiebacks are also a good place for machine-embroidered designs (pages 50 and 51).

Consider the size of the window or shower curtain when choosing the size of the cording for shirred tiebacks. Because these tiebacks are circular, they can simply be slipped onto the curtain from the bottom and secured with one hook. To determine the finished length of either style tieback, draw the curtain back to the desired position, and measure with a cloth tape measure.

The position of the tiebacks on the window curtain affects the amount of exposed glass as well as the overall look of the curtains. Position tiebacks low to cover more of the window and to visually widen the window. If tiebacks are positioned high, more of the glass is exposed and visual height is added to the window. Also follow these guidelines for positioning the tiebacks on a stationary shower curtain, allowing enough room for easy access to the tub.

MATERIALS

Fabric that matches or contrasts with the curtain fabric.

Fusible interfacing, optional embellishments, such as fabric bands (page 117) or galloon lace (page 113), for tiebacks with tucked ends.

Cording in desired diameter, for shirred tiebacks.

Sew-on or pin-on tieback rings.

Tiebacks with tucked ends have clean, simple design lines. Machine-embroidered airplane motifs (opposite) fly along the tucked-end tieback in a child's bedroom. The tieback at right is trimmed with fabric bands as on page 117.

Shirred tiebacks (left) mimic the effect created at the heading of rod-pocket curtains (page 63).

Making
Shirred Tiebacks

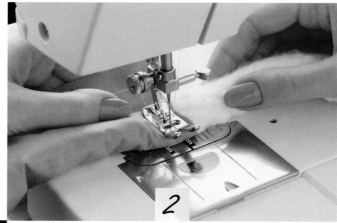

1 Cut a length of cording for each tieback with length equal to three times the finished circumference of tieback; wrap tape around ends to prevent fraying. Cut fabric strip for each tieback with length equal to twice the finished tieback circumference and width equal to cording circumference plus 2" (5 cm).

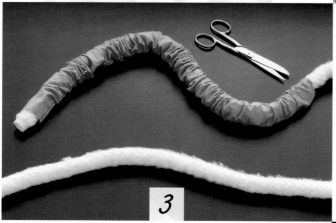

2 Fold fabric strip in half lengthwise, right sides together, encasing the cording; stitch ½" (1.3 cm) seam. Stitch across end of fabric strip through cording.

3 Hold fabric loosely at stitched end; pull fabric from the covered to the uncovered end of cording, turning tube right side out to encase the cording and gathering fabric as tube is turned. Cut off and discard excess cording.

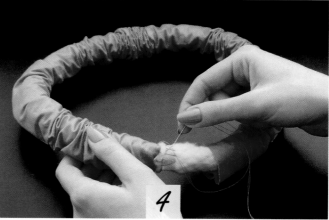

4 Sew the ends of the cording together securely.

5 Turn under ½" (1.3 cm) at the end of the fabric tube. Overlap the stitched end of the covered cord; slipstitch in place. Distribute fabric evenly along the cording. Attach a tieback ring.

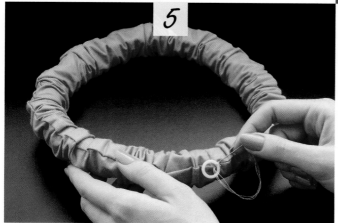

Making
Tiebacks with Tucked Ends

1 Cut fabric strip for each tieback 1" (2.5 cm) longer than desired finished length, with width of fabric strip equal to twice the desired finished width plus 1" (2.5 cm). Cut strip of fusible interfacing for each tieback to the desired finished length and width of tieback. Center strip of fusible interfacing on the wrong side of fabric strip, and fuse in place, following the manufacturer's directions. The right side of the interfaced area will be the front of the tieback.

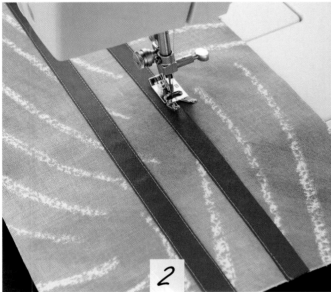

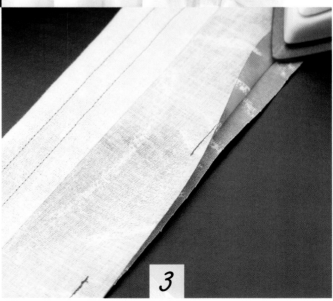

2 Apply any desired embellishments to right side of the tieback in the interfaced area, such as the fabric bands (page 117) shown.

3 Fold the tieback in half, right sides together. Stitch ½" (1.3 cm) lengthwise seam, leaving opening for turning. Press seam open.

Continued

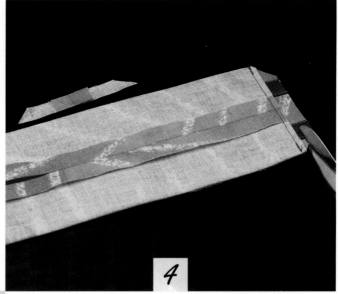

4

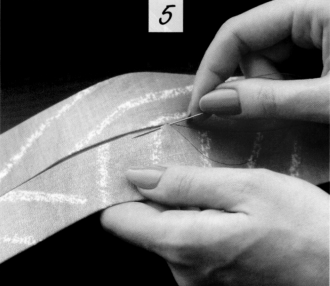

5

4 Center seam on back of tieback. Stitch ½"
(1.3 cm) seams at the ends; trim seam
allowances, and clip corners.

5 Turn the tieback right side out, and press.
Slipstitch the opening closed.

6 Fold one end of the tieback in half, right
sides together. Stitch a tuck, 1" (2.5 cm) long
and ⅜" (1 cm) from fold, starting 1" (2.5 cm)
from end of tieback. Repeat for opposite end.

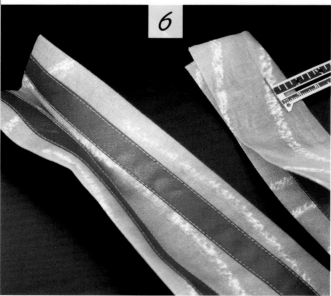

6

7 Flatten the tuck, centering it over the stitches.

8 Stitch in the ditch of the tuck from the right side, to hold it in place. Repeat for the opposite end.

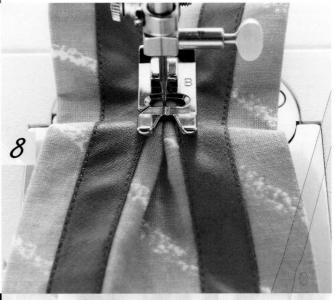

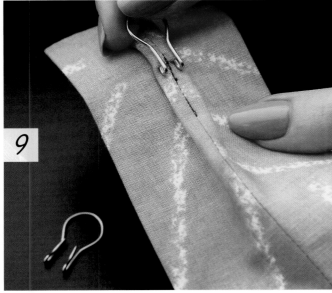

9 Attach pin-on tieback rings as shown. Or stitch sew-on tieback rings in place.

Decorative metal rods with ornate finials
enhance the window treatment. They are available in many sizes, styles, and colors, complete
with coordinating wall brackets.

Curtain
HARDWARE

When you are choosing a shower curtain or window treatment style for the bathroom or bedroom, also consider the selection of hardware that is available. If the treatment will be hung from rings, it requires a decorative rod; select from a variety of metal and wood rods and pole sets. In the bathroom, you may want to use shiny chrome or brass hardware to carry out the look of the faucets and other fixtures. If the rod will be concealed in a rod pocket, select either bracket-mounted or spring-tension curtain rods in one of three widths or plain wooden poles.

The rods for window treatments are installed with a pair of wall-mount brackets that project out from the wall or window frame. If the screws are not inserted into wall studs, support them with plastic sleeves, plastic toggle anchors, or molly bolts, depending on the weight of the treatment.

Shower bars are usually installed between the side walls of the shower opening by using a rod with socket-style brackets or a spring-tension rod without brackets. If the brackets will be installed on a ceramic tile wall, you may drill into the ceramic tile with a glass-and-tile drill bit and insert a plastic anchor into the hole before you install the bracket. Or use an adhesive mounting plate (page 77) to eliminate the need for drilling into the ceramic tile.

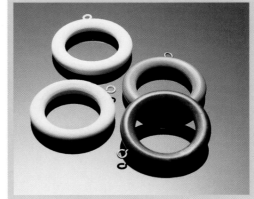

Metal rings and hooks (top, left), sold in sets of twelve for shower curtains or purchased separately, are available in brass, nickel, iron, and chrome. The styles range from simple utility rings to ornamental designs.

Wooden rings (top, right) can be used as shower curtain rings with a wooden pole. They may also be used for window curtains hung from a wooden pole. The rings may be stained or painted to match the pole.

Molded plastic rings (right), available in several colors, snap open and closed. They are also sold in sets of twelve.

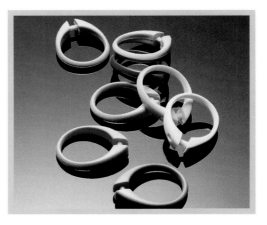

More Curtain
Hardware

Oval curtain rods, 1″ (2.5 cm) wide, are used to hang rod-pocket window treatments. For rod-pocket shower curtains, spring-tension oval rods are also available.

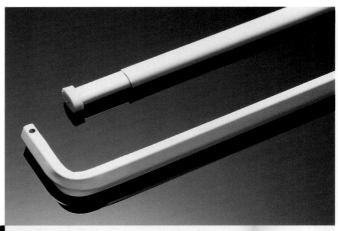

Shower bars, sold with end plates, are available in brass and chrome. The end plates are screwed into the side walls of the shower opening.

Wide curtain rods are available in both 2½″ and 4½″ (6.5 and 11.5 cm) widths. They add depth and interest to rod-pocket window treatments. Both these widths are available in wall-mount rods for window treatments and in spring-tension rods for shower curtains.

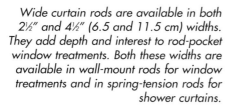

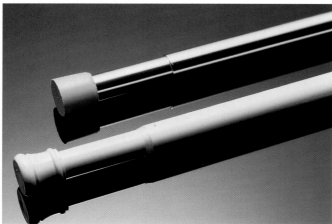

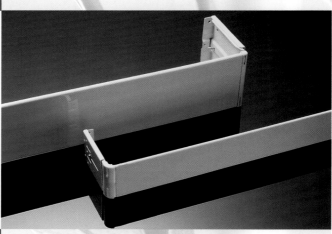

Round spring-tension rods are available in several diameters and finishes. They may be used for shower curtains or inside-mounted window treatments, such as cafe curtains. Because no mounting brackets are needed, the window frames and shower walls are not damaged by screws.

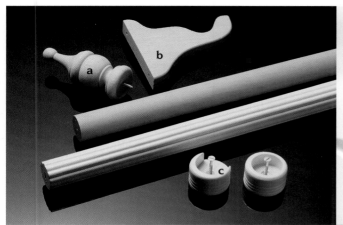

Wooden poles are available unfinished and in several finishes. For a window treatment, finials (a) are attached to the ends of the pole, and wooden brackets (b) are used for mounting the pole. When used as a shower bar, the pole is mounted with wooden sockets (c); these sockets may be stained or painted to match the pole. Wooden rings are also available.

Adhesive mounting kits are used to mount shower bars, making it unnecessary to drill holes in ceramic tiles. The mounting plate is affixed to the tile with a double-stick adhesive disk, and the rod brackets screw into the plate.

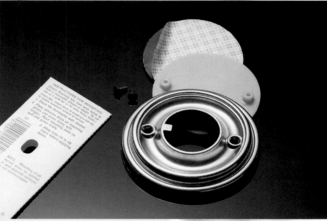

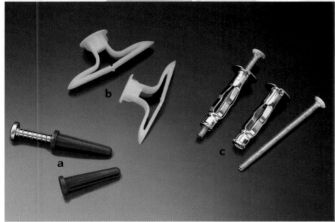

Plastic sleeves (a), plastic toggle anchors (b), and molly bolts (c) are used to support wall brackets for curtain rods and poles when the screws do not enter wall studs or the window frame.

Tieback holders are used to keep the tiebacks of shower curtains and window treatments in place. For mounting on drywall or woodwork, use either tenter hooks (a) or cup hooks (b). For mounting on ceramic tile, use adhesive plastic hooks (c).

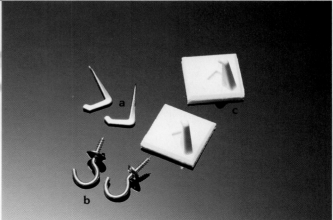

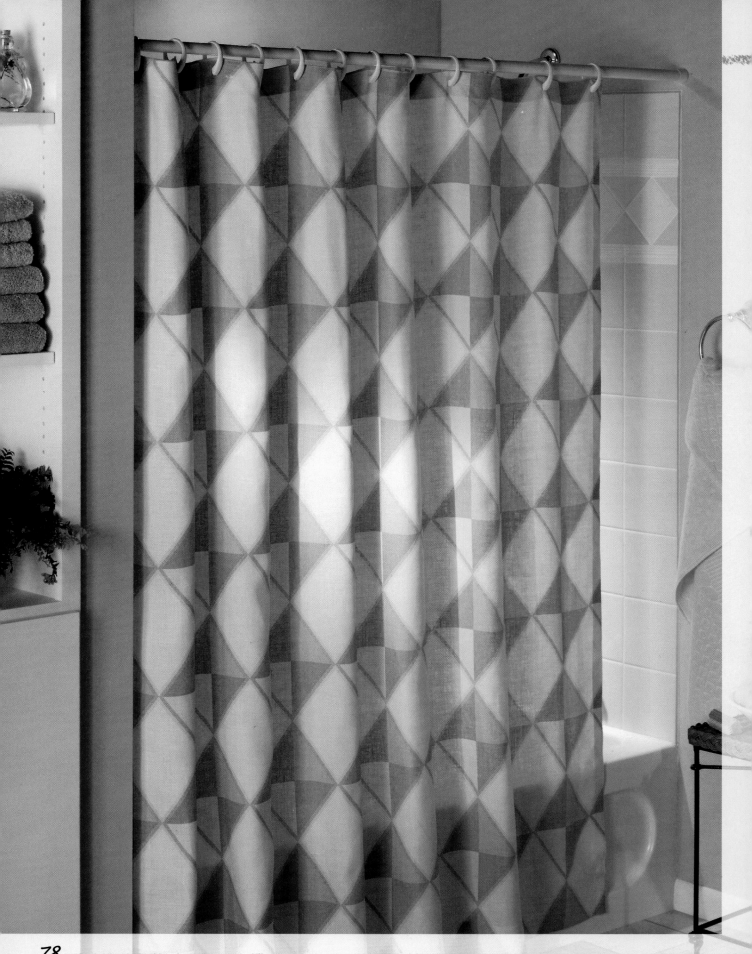

Basic Shower CURTAINS

Sewing a shower curtain for your bathroom allows you more flexibility in fabric selection than if you purchase one ready-made. Make a basic curtain that matches or coordinates with the fabrics in an adjoining bedroom. Or make shower and window curtains in complementary styles and matching fabrics.

The basic shower curtain has twelve grommets or buttonholes at the top, spaced to match the holes along the top of a shower curtain liner, so that the curtain and liner can be hung together on the same rod. A separate valance, constructed like the curtain, may be added and hung together with the curtain and liner. Or the valance may be attached to the shower curtain.

A basic shower curtain measures 72" (183 cm) long and 72" (183 cm) wide, to be used with a standard liner, and is usually mounted so the lower edge is about 2" (5 cm) from the floor. Valances range in length up to 15" (38 cm). The curtain can be made longer than 72" (183 cm), if desired, but, to ensure that the curtain, valance, and liner hang together properly, do not alter the recommended width of either the curtain or valance.

For easy laundering, choose a fabric that is washable, and preshrink it before sewing the curtain by washing and drying the fabric according to the manufacturer's directions. Avoid using decorator fabrics with polished finishes, because they are usually not washable and any water that is splashed on the decorator fabric can leave noticeable spots.

MATERIALS

4⅝ yd. (4.25 m) fabric, for curtain; 1¼ yd. (1.15 m) fabric for valance. Allow extra fabric for matching patterns.

Twelve grommets and attaching tool, optional.

Shower curtain liner.

Shower bar extension rod and twelve rings.

Basic shower curtains may be used alone, as shown opposite, or with either a separate or an attached valance. The valance at right, sewn from a contrasting fabric, is stitched to the top of the curtain.

BASIC SHOWER CURTAIN

Basic curtain with optional separate valance:

For standard size curtain 72" × 72" (183 × 183 cm), cut length is 82" (208.5 cm). Cut width* (after piecing) is 76" (193 cm).

Longer curtain:

Measure desired finished length:
Add 10" (25.5 cm) + 10"
to find cut length of both pieces. =

Separate valance:

Measure desired finished length:
Add 6" (15 cm) + 6"
to find cut length for both pieces. =
Cut width* (after piecing) is 76" (193 cm).

Curtain with attached valance:

For standard size curtain 72" × 72" (183 × 183 cm), cut length is 78" (198 cm). Cut width* (after piecing) is 76" (193 cm).

Longer curtain:

Measure desired finished length:
Add 6" (15 cm) + 6"
to find cut length of both pieces. =

Attached valance:

Measure desired finished length:
Add 4½" (11.5 cm) + 4½"
to find cut length of both pieces. =
Cut width* (after piecing) is 76" (193 cm).

*Shower curtains and valances require one full width of fabric and one partial width. Trim to necessary cut width after piecing.

Sewing a
Basic Shower Curtain with an Optional Separate Valance

1 Pin fabric widths for curtain panel, wrong sides together; stitch scant ¼" (6 mm) seam. Press seam allowances to one side.

2 Fold the fabric along the seamline, right sides together, enclosing seam allowances; press.

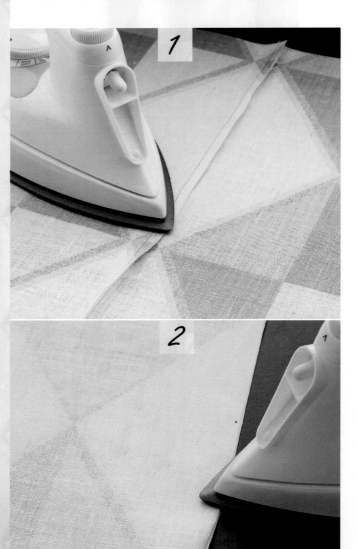

3 Stitch ⅜" (1 cm) from folded edge, enclosing first seam. Press French seam to one side.

4 Trim curtain panel to 76" (193 cm) wide, trimming one side of the panel. Press under 3" (7.5 cm) twice on lower edge of curtain panel; stitch to make 3" (7.5 cm) double-fold hem.

5 Press under 1" (2.5 cm) twice on each side of the curtain panel; stitch to make 1" (2.5 cm) double-fold side hems.

6 Press under and stitch 2" (5 cm) double-fold hem on upper edge of curtain panel.

Continued

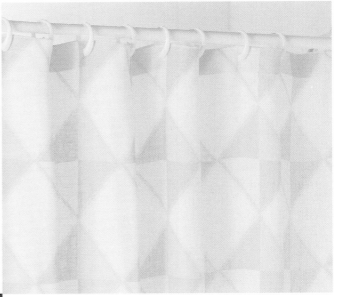

Sewing a
Basic Shower Curtain with an
Optional Separate Valance
(continued)

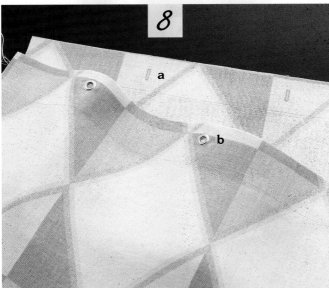

7 Mark the curtain panel for the placement of twelve buttonholes or grommets, a scant 6" (15 cm) apart and ¾" (2 cm) down from the top, with end marks 1½" (3.8 cm) from the sides.

8 Make ½" (1.3 cm) buttonholes **(a),** if desired, stitching them vertically with upper ends at the placement marks. Or fasten grommets **(b)** securely, following the manufacturer's directions, centering the grommets on the placement marks.

Valance. Construct the valance as on pages 80 to 82, steps 1 to 7, except, in step 4, press and stitch a 1" (2.5 cm) double-fold lower hem. Attach shower curtain rings to the tops of curtain and valance, through both layers, as shown.

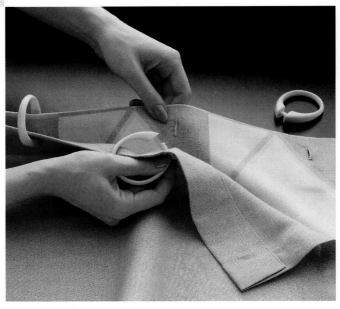

Sewing a
Basic Shower Curtain with an Attached Valance

1 Seam the fabric widths together for curtain panel and for valance panel; if desired, stitch French seams, pages 80 and 81, steps 1 to 3. Follow step 4, for the curtain; for the valance, follow step 4, except press and stitch 1" (2.5 cm) double-fold lower hem. On upper edge of valance, press under ½" (1.3 cm), then 2" (5 cm).

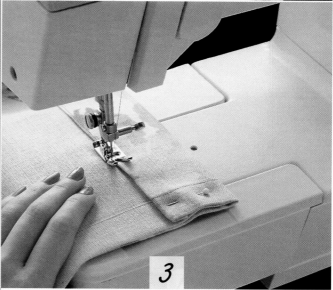

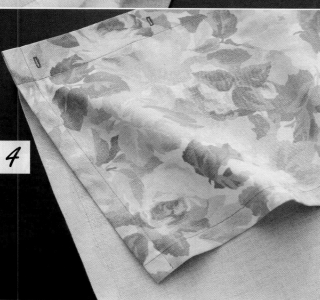

2 Place the valance right side down on flat surface. Place curtain right side down over valance, with upper edge of the curtain even with folded edge of the valance; pin in place.

3 Stitch along lower fold, catching the curtain between layers of valance.

4 Mark and apply buttonholes or grommets as in steps 6 and 7, opposite.

Shower Curtains with

TUCKED BORDERS

In this variation of a basic shower curtain, design interest is created at the lower edge. A series of three 1" (2.5 cm) tucks, spaced 1" (2.5 cm) apart, is sewn at the lower edge, with the hem edge stitched into the first tuck. When the shower curtain is made from a simple cotton or linen fabric, the crisp tucks add a handsome border.

MATERIALS	
Lightweight decorator fabric.	
Twelve grommets and attaching tool, optional.	
Shower curtain liner.	
Shower curtain rod and twelve rings.	

Tucks sewn above the hem of a pinstriped linen shower curtain (opposite) add tailored, understated detailing.

Repeat the tucked border on sheer bedroom curtains (right) for a coordinated look.

Shower Curtain with a Tucked Border

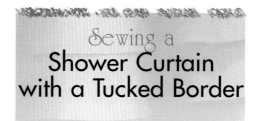

TUCKED-BORDER SHOWER CURTAIN

For standard size curtain 72" × 72" (183 × 183 cm), cut length is 88" (223.5 cm) and the cut width* is 76" (193 cm).

Longer curtain:

Measure desired finished length:

      Add 16" (40.5 cm)   + 16"

to find cut length of both pieces.   =

*Shower curtains require one full width of fabric and one partial width. Trim to necessary cut width after piecing.

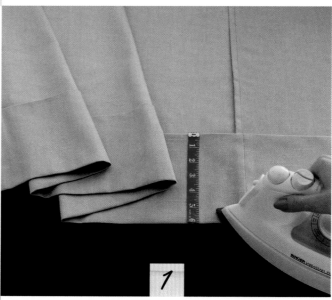

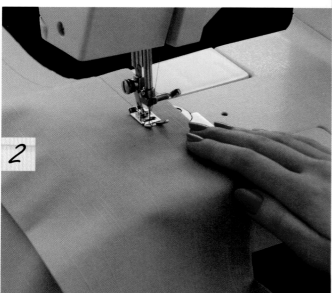

1 Seam fabric widths together. At lower edge, press under 6" (15 cm) twice to wrong side of fabric.

2 Stitch a tuck 1" (2.5 cm) from the second foldline, catching the lower edge inside the tuck. Press the tuck toward lower edge of the curtain panel.

3 Press the foldline for second tuck to wrong side of the fabric, 3" (7.5 cm) above stitching line. Press the foldline for third tuck to the wrong side, 4" (10 cm) above foldline for second tuck.

4 Stitch tucks 1" (2.5 cm) from foldlines. Press tucks toward the lower edge of curtain panel.

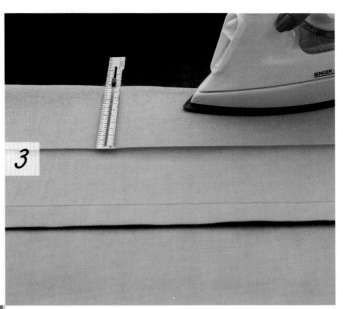

5 Press under and stitch 1" (2.5 cm) double-fold hem on each side of curtain panel.

6 Complete the shower curtain as for the basic curtain on pages 81 and 82, steps 5 to 7.

Curtains with DRAPED HEADINGS

A heading of matching or contrasting fabric drapes gracefully along the top of this curtain. Suitable for both shower curtains and window treatments, these curtains may be hung with sewn-on rings. Or apply buttonholes or grommets for use with hooks or snap-on rings.

When mounting the rod for a shower curtain, position the lower edge of the rod about 10" (25.5 cm) above the rod for the liner, so the liner does not show in the swooped areas between the rings. When mounting the rod for a window treatment, position the rod about 10" (25.5 cm) above the molding to keep the top of the window from showing.

Made from lightweight fabric that drapes softly, the curtain and the heading have two times fullness with the rings or hooks spaced 12" to 16" (30.5 to 40.5 cm) apart. If you prefer to use less fullness in the curtain or to space the rings closer together, the depth of the swoops will be shortened and the rod may be hung lower. Before permanently installing the rod, hang the curtain on it and hold it in place to check the height. If you are making a matching shower curtain and window treatment, you may be able to hang them both at the same height.

MATERIALS

Lightweight fabric that drapes softly, for the curtain; matching or contrasting lightweight, soft fabric may be used for the heading.

Grommets and attaching tool, optional.

Wooden pole with sewn-on wooden rings, or shower bar or curtain rod with hooks or snap-on rings.

Lightweight crinkled fabric drapes into deep swoops (opposite) for a relaxed look.

King-size bed sheet is used for the shower curtain at right.

CURTAIN WITH A DRAPED HEADING

Curtain:

Measure desired finished length from bottom of rod to floor:	
Subtract 1" (2.5 cm)	− 1"
for curtain that clears floor by 2" (5 cm)	OR
OR add 3" (7.5 cm)	+ 3"
for curtain that breaks at the floor to find cut length of the pieces.	=
Measure the rod length:	
Multiply by 2 times fullness	× 2
to find cut width (after piecing).	=
Divide by the fabric width	÷
to find number of widths needed; round up to the next whole number.	=
Multiply by the cut length	×
to find total amount of fabric needed.	=

Heading:

Cut length is 29" (73.5 cm).	
Determine cut width of curtain (above):	
Subtract 3" (7.5 cm)	− 3"
to find cut width (after piecing).	=
Divide by the fabric width	÷
to find number of widths needed; round up to the next whole number.	=
Multiply by the cut length (29" [73.5 cm])	× 29"
to find total amount of fabric needed.	=

Curtain with a Draped Heading

1 Seam the fabric widths together; if desired, stitch French seams, as on pages 80 and 81, steps 1 to 3. Press under 3" (7.5 cm) twice on lower edge of curtain panel; stitch to make 3" (7.5 cm) double-fold hem. Press under 1" (2.5 cm) twice on each side of the curtain panel; stitch to make 1" (2.5 cm) double-fold side hems.

2 Seam fabric widths together for heading, using ½" (1.3 cm) conventional seams; French seams are not used. Press seams open. Fold the heading in half lengthwise, right sides together; at ends, stitch ½" (1.3 cm) seams.

3 Turn the heading right side out; press the seams at ends. Baste the raw edges together; press along the fold.

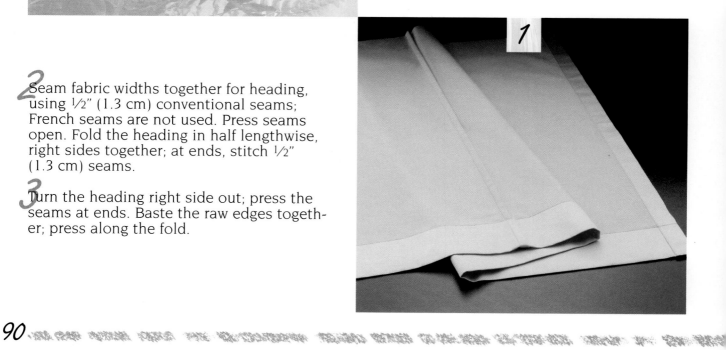

1

4 Pin the heading to the top of the curtain panel, matching raw edges, with the right side of the heading facing down on the wrong side of the curtain panel. Stitch ½" (1.3 cm) seam; finish the seam, using zigzag or overlock stitch.

5 Fold the heading 3" (7.5 cm) above seamline as shown. Pin in place; do not press foldline.

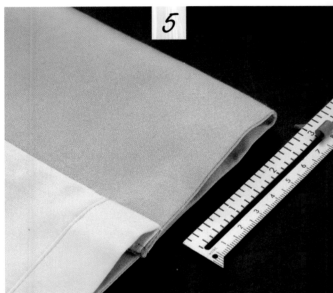

6 Mark the fold at the upper edge, ½" (1.3 cm) from each side of the curtain panel, to mark placement for end rings. Mark placement for the remaining rings, about 12" to 16" (30.5 to 40.5 cm) apart, dividing the distance between end marks evenly.

7 Sew rings to the back side of heading at markings, using small stitches around entire metal eye **(a).** Or stitch buttonholes **(b)** or attach grommets **(c),** with the top of each buttonhole or grommet ½" (1.3 cm) below the fold at the upper edge; stitch buttonholes or attach grommets through all four layers of heading and curtain panel.

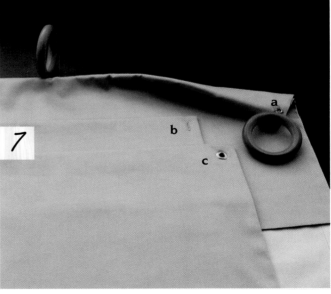

Banded Shower CURTAINS

For a striking, tailored effect, make a shower curtain with contrasting banded edges. Combine two solid-colored fabrics to give a simple, yet dramatic, look. Or use a patterned fabric with a coordinating solid.

The instructions that follow are for a standard shower curtain that measures 72" (183 cm) long and 72" (183 cm) wide. To eliminate any seams, the band strips are cut on the lengthwise grain. The curtain can be hung together with a standard shower curtain liner, using one shower bar and one set of rings.

MATERIALS

4½ yd. (4.15 m) fabric, for the curtain.

2¼ yd. (2.1 m) fabric, for the bands.

Twelve grommets and attaching tool, optional.

Shower curtain liner.

Shower bar and twelve rings.

BANDED SHOWER CURTAIN

WORKSHEET

Shower curtain:

Cut length is 76½" (194.3 cm).
Cut width* after piecing is 73" (185.5 cm).

Bands:

Cut length of side bands is 76½" (194.3 cm).
Cut length for lower band is 73" (185.5 cm).
Determine desired finished width:
Add 1" (2.5 cm) + 1"
to find cut width of bands. =

*Shower curtain requires one full width of fabric and one partial width. Trim to necessary cut width after piecing.

Sewing a
Banded Shower Curtain

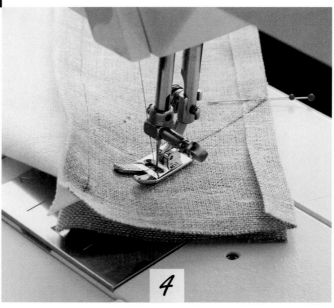

1 Seam the fabric widths together, using French seams, pages 80 and 81, steps 1 to 3. Trim curtain panel to 73" (185.5 cm) wide, trimming one side of the panel. Press under 1/2" (1.3 cm) on one long edge of one side band. Pin band to curtain panel, with right side of band to wrong side of panel. Stitch a 1/2" (1.3 cm) seam, stopping 1/2" (1.3 cm) from lower edge. Repeat for band on opposite side.

2 Press under 1/2" (1.3 cm) on one long edge of lower band. Pin to lower edge of curtain panel, with right side of band to wrong side of panel. Stitch 1/2" (1.3 cm) seam; start and stop 1/2" (1.3 cm) from side edges.

3 Mark band for mitering, placing pins at inner corner as shown.

4 Stitch miters, from pin marks at inner corner to end of stitching at outer corner; take care not to catch the curtain panel in stitching.

5 Trim mitered seams to ¼" (6 mm), and press open. Trim the corners diagonally.

6 Press seams open by pressing seam allowance of band toward band, using tip of iron.

7 Turn band to right side of curtain; press band, with the seamline on outer edge of curtain.

8 Pin the band in place. Stitch around the band, close to the inner fold.

9 Complete the shower curtain as for the basic curtain on pages 81 and 82, steps 5 to 7.

Ideas for
SHOWER CURTAINS

Design features used elsewhere in the bathroom and bedroom can be repeated on the shower curtain, unifying the scheme. Coordinated fabrics used for window curtains and shower curtains are an obvious place to start. Finishing touches might include fabric bands, bindings, decorative trims, embroidery, or reverse appliqués.

Contrasting fabric bands (page 117) are stitched on the valance at far left, adding interest to the basic shower curtain and perhaps echoing a towel embellishment.

The lower edge of this shower curtain valance (near left) is scalloped and bound (page 116). Because the scallops are wider apart, they can also be made deeper than is recommended for towels. Ties are made as on page 45, step 1.

Wide lace edging embellishes the lower edge of the shower curtain above. The lace is applied, adding a taffeta band along the upper edge of the lace, as on page 113.

Child's handprints are applied to the banded shower curtain (left) (page 93). Dilute the fabric paint slightly with water in a shallow pan. Then dip the child's hand in the paint, and place it on the fabric, pressing down on the fingers and palm. Heat-set the fabric paint according to the manufacturer's directions.

Sink & Vanity SKIRTS

By adding a gathered skirt to the bathroom sink or a vanity table, you can introduce the softness of fabric into the bathroom or repeat a fabric that has been used for a window treatment or shower curtain. The sink skirt can conceal unsightly plumbing while creating a hidden storage area that is easily accessible. Attaching a skirt to a small table can transform it into a vanity with room for storing baskets of cosmetics and toiletries under the skirt.

For easy cleaning, make the skirt from a washable fabric and attach it to the sink or vanity table with hook and loop tape. If you will be laundering the skirt, preshrink the fabric before cutting the pieces.

Usually, sink and vanity skirts are applied to the outer surface, extending from wall to wall. For some styles of wall-mount sinks, you may want to apply the skirt to the inner surface and extend it around the back for a few inches (centimeters). If the sink or table stands away from the wall, or is round or oval in shape, you may want to apply the skirt completely around it.

MATERIALS

Fabric; find amount by multiplying number of pieces (step 2) by the cut length of each piece (step 3).

Sew-on hook and loop tape, ¾" (2 cm) wide, in length equal to finished width of skirt (step 2).

Adhesive designed for use with hook and loop tape.

Vanity table skirt (opposite), applied to the outer surface of the apron, transforms a table into a vanity.

Sink skirt (right) adds softness to the decorating scheme of the bathroom and conceals any exposed plumbing.

Making a
Sink or Vanity Skirt

1 Decide where you want the hook and loop tape, for either outside or inside mount; mark a placement line on sink or table, parallel to the floor. Apply hook side of hook and loop tape to sink or table; affix tape with adhesive designed for the hook and loop tape, according to the manufacturer's directions.

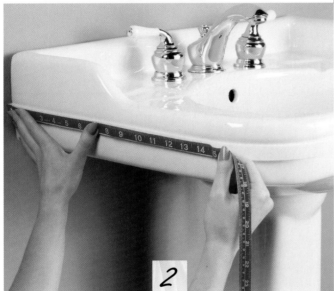

2 Secure loop side of hook and loop tape over hook side. Determine finished width of skirt by measuring around sink or vanity where skirt will be attached; measure over the tape on outside or inside. Multiply by 2½ times fullness; divide by fabric width to determine number of pieces to cut.

3 Measure for the finished length of the skirt, from the lower edge of the tape to the floor; subtract ½" (1.3 cm) from this measurement, to allow for clearance at the floor. Add 2½" (6.5 cm) to determine the cut length of each piece. Cut the pieces. Cut one 3" (7.5 cm) fabric strip for the band, with the length of the strip equal to the desired finished width of the skirt plus 1" (2.5 cm).

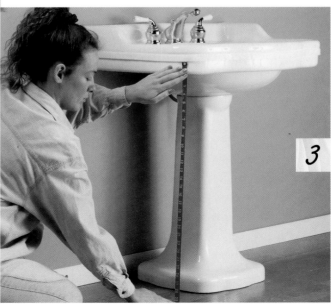

4 Press under 1" (2.5 cm) twice on the lower edge of the skirt; stitch to make 1" (2.5 cm) double-fold hem. Press under and stitch ½" (1.3 cm) double-fold hems on sides of skirt.

5 Zigzag over a cord at the upper edge of the skirt, within seam allowance, just beyond seamline, on wrong side of fabric.

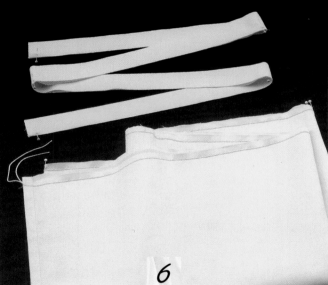

6 Divide upper edge of the skirt into fourths; pin-mark. Press the band in half lengthwise, matching the long edges. Pin-mark one long edge of the band ½" (1.3 cm) from each end; divide the distance between pins into fourths, and pin-mark. Unfold the band.

7 Pin skirt to the band, right sides together, matching pin marks. Pull up gathering cord, and gather skirt evenly to fit. Pin in place.

Continued

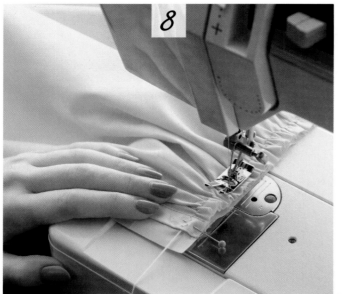

8 Stitch the band to the skirt in ½" (1.3 cm) seam. Press seam allowances toward the band.

9 Position loop side of hook and loop tape on band, ⅛" (3 mm) from pressed line; place the tape on back of band if the skirt will be applied to outside surface of sink or table, or place on front of band if the skirt will be applied to inside surface. Stitch along both long edges of tape.

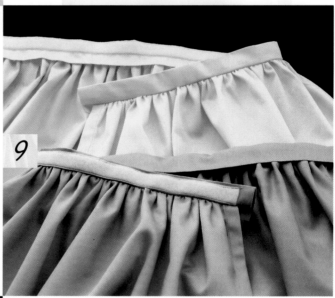

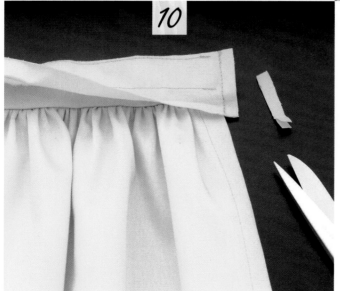

10 Press under ⅜" (1 cm) on the remaining long edge of band. Fold band, right sides together, along pressed centerline. Stitch ½" (1.3 cm) seams at ends; trim.

11 Turn band right side out, enclosing seam allowances; press ends. From the right side of skirt, pin the band in place along seamline, catching the lower edge of band on wrong side.

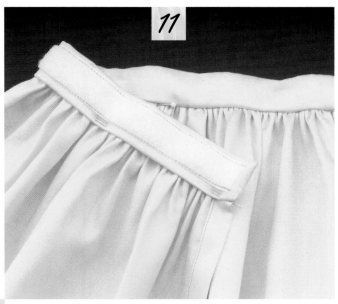

12 Stitch in the ditch from the right side by stitching in the well of the seam. Attach skirt, using an outside or inside mount.

Inside attachment. Attach the skirt to the inner surface, if possible, using hook and loop tape.

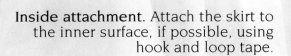

Fringed-fabric RUGS

Fringed-fabric rugs with a thick, plush nap make comfortable bath mats or area rugs for the bedroom. Design and sew them in any size and color combination to match your decor. They are easy care; occasional machine washing and drying restores their fluffiness.

For best results, select washable lightweight to mediumweight woven cotton fabrics, such as broadcloth or sheeting. Cotton is comfortable and absorbent and will curl, fray, and wrinkle when washed, giving your rug wonderful texture. Some cotton blends can be used, though they will not curl and wrinkle as much as the cottons. Avoid loosely woven fabrics that may fray excessively, and, because both sides of the fabric are exposed, avoid printed fabrics that have an obvious wrong side. Flawed or off-grain fabrics may be used, however, because the final appearance of the rug depends primarily on its fiber content and color.

Cotton canvas or cotton drill, most readily available in white or off-white, is used for the backing fabric. The fringed fabric is fairly dense, though you may see occasional glimpses of the backing fabric. If the fringe fabrics are dark or bright in color and a coordinating canvas backing is unavailable, you may want to layer a coordinating fabric over the backing before you start sewing the fringe strips in place.

Use the worksheet on page 106 to calculate the total number of fabric strips you need for the rug. Then decide how many of these strips you want to cut from each fabric, depending on your color selection and the desired appearance.

For safety, place a purchased nonslip pad between the rug and the floor.

MATERIALS

Lightweight to mediumweight cotton or cotton-blend fabrics, for the cut fringe.

Heavy cotton canvas or drill, for the backing.

Fabric to cover the backing, optional.

Nonslip pad, to place under the finished rug.

Oval rug (opposite) combines several colors of hand-dyed fabric in 100 percent cotton.

Rectangular rug (right) has assorted solids and yarn-dyed plaids with a subtle color variation.

CALCULATING THE FABRIC FOR THE FRINGE

Determine finished width of the rug: Multiply by 2	× 2
to find total number of inner rows.	=
Add 2 for the outer rows	+ 2
to find total number of rows.	=
Multiply this number by the desired finished length of the rug	×
to find total length of strips needed for rectangular or square rug.	=
Add the distance around perimeter for an oval or round rug	+
to find total length of strips needed for an oval or round rug.	=
Divide the total strip length by the fabric width	÷
to find total number of strips to cut; round up to next whole number.*	=
Multiply this number by 5" (12.5 cm) (the width of the strips)	× 5"
to find total amount of fabric to buy.	=

*The total amount of fabric may be divided among several fabrics, for a multicolored or multitextured look.

Making a
Rectangular or Square Fringed Rug

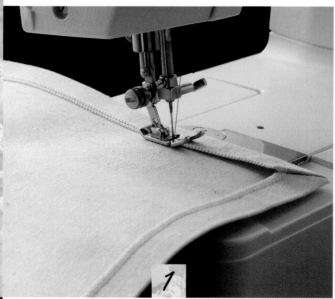

1 Cut canvas or drill backing 1½" (3.8 cm) longer and wider than desired finished size. Cut fabric to cover backing, if desired, to same size as backing; pin it to right side of backing. Finish raw edges of the backing. Press ¾" (2 cm) hem allowances to wrong side; stitch in place.

2 Draw lengthwise placement lines on right side of backing, ½" (1.3 cm) apart.

3 Trim selvages from the fringe fabrics. Cut 5" (12.5 cm) fabric strips across the width of fabric; refer to worksheet for approximate number of fabric strips needed. Press the fabric strips in half lengthwise, matching raw edges.

4 Stitch first fabric strip to backing, with folded edge of strip just covering one long edge of backing and with raw edges extending out from backing.

5 Trim off excess fabric strip at end, even with edge of backing.

6 Stitch next fabric strip to backing, with the folded edge on the first placement line and with strip facing in same direction as first row. At end, trim the strip even with edge of backing.

7 Repeat step 6 for subsequent rows. To add another strip within a row, butt end of new strip to previous strip, and continue stitching.

Continued

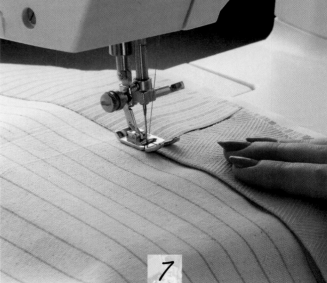

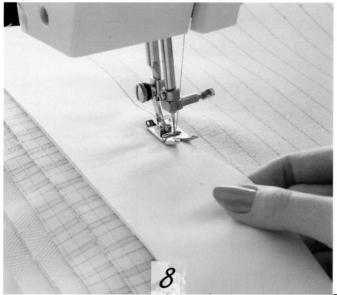

8 Rotate rug in opposite direction when about one-half of the rows are completed, to eliminate bulk of fabric under the head of the sewing machine. Stitch remaining rows, with strips facing in same direction as first half of rows.

9 Stitch last fabric strip with folded edge even with hemmed edge of backing.

10 Cut the fabric strips through both layers at 1/2" (1.3 cm) intervals, cutting up to 1/2" (1.3 cm) from fold. When cutting, fold all remaining fabric out of the way and place a straightedge under the strip you are cutting.

11 Machine wash and machine dry rug several times, to achieve frayed and curled look.

Making a
Round or Oval
Fringed Rug

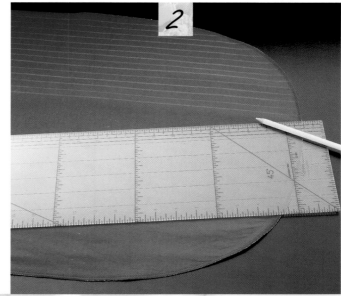

1 Cut canvas or drill backing to finished size. Pin a layer of fabric over the backing, if necessary. Finish raw edges.

2 Mark placement lines on right side of the backing, along straight of grain, ½" (1.3 cm) apart; on an oval rug, mark the lines lengthwise. Press the fabric strips as on page 107, step 3.

3 Stitch first fabric strip around backing, with the folded edge of the strip overlapping the edge of backing ¼" (6 mm) and with raw edges extending out from backing. Ease strip to backing as you sew, by pushing small tucks in strip with pin; do not stitch over pins.

4 Butt ends of fabric strips together if more than one strip is needed, and butt strips at beginning and end of circle.

5 Stitch the remaining rows as on pages 107 and 108, steps 6 to 8, except trim fabric strips at ends so they overlap the outer fabric strip ¼" (6 mm). Complete rug as in steps 10 and 11, opposite.

Decorative TOWELS

A few minutes at the sewing machine can turn ordinary towels into high-style decorator accents for your bathroom. Encase silk flowers under sheer organdy (opposite) for a fresh, delicate look. Create fine detailing with appliqués, fabric bands or bindings, decorative braids, and lace trims. Or add your personal touch with elegant machine-embroidered motifs and monograms.

For embellishing towels, select lightweight to mediumweight washable fabrics. Polyester taffetas and satins are good choices for bands, binding, and appliqués, because they have a subtle sheen, hold their shape, and launder well. Select cotton, nylon, or polyester laces, such as eyelets, Schiffli, or Cluny lace in galloon or edging styles. Check decorative braids to be sure they are also washable. Ease laces and trims slightly as they are being applied, to allow the towel to fold back smoothly after embellishing.

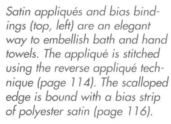

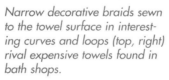

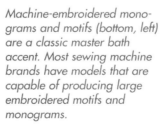

Silk flowers (opposite) captured between layers of sheer polyester organza (page 112) are accented with a coordinating ribbon.

Satin appliqués and bias bindings (top, left) are an elegant way to embellish bath and hand towels. The appliqué is stitched using the reverse appliqué technique (page 114). The scalloped edge is bound with a bias strip of polyester satin (page 116).

Narrow decorative braids sewn to the towel surface in interesting curves and loops (top, right) rival expensive towels found in bath shops.

Machine-embroidered monograms and motifs (bottom, left) are a classic master bath accent. Most sewing machine brands have models that are capable of producing large embroidered motifs and monograms.

Lace trim (page 113) may be added as an edging along the lower edge of a towel or as a band across the width (bottom, right). Fabric band conceals upper edge of lace edging.

Floating Flowers in
Organza

1 Remove silk flower petals and leaves from stems. Soak in mild suds, rinse, and allow to dry, to prevent color bleeding.

2 Trim away towel border, if necessary; finish edge, using zigzag or serger. Cut sheer fabric 1" (2.5 cm) wider than towel width and twice the desired length plus ½" (1.3 cm) for seam allowances. Lightly press sheer fabric in half. Plan flower placement on one half of sheer fabric, with back of flowers to wrong side of fabric. Secure with small hand stitches. Stitch small pearl at each flower center, if desired.

3 Press under ¼" (6 mm) on long edge opposite flowers. Pin unpressed edge of border, right side down, to back of towel. Stitch ¼" (6 mm) seam; finish seam allowance, using zigzag or serger.

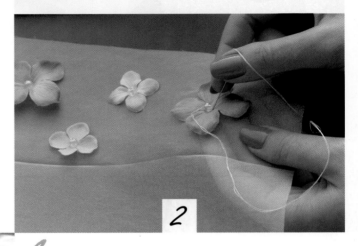

4 Fold border back, right sides together, matching outer edges. Stitch ends even with sides of towel; avoid catching towel in stitches. Trim seam allowances to ¼" (6 mm), and finish.

5 Turn border right side out; press. Place folded edge over lower front edge of towel, matching fold to seamline. Topstitch close to fold. If additional detailing is desired, cover the upper edge with a bias fabric band (page 117) or purchased trim.

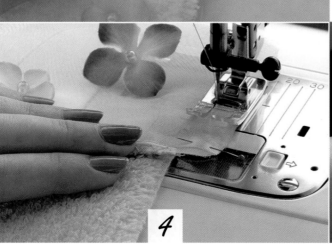

Applying
Lace

MATERIALS

Purchased plain towel.

Galloon lace or lace edging.

Washable mediumweight fabric, such as polyester satin or taffeta, if fabric band is desired.

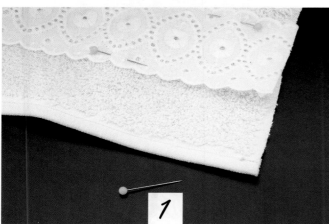

1 **Galloon lace.** Cut lace 1″ (2.5 cm) longer than width of towel. Turn under ½″ (1.3 cm) at ends; pin lace in place at the desired distance above lower edge of towel.

2 Stitch along folded ends and both scalloped edges of the lace, using straight stitch.

Lace edging. Follow step 1, above, except pin lace so it covers lower edge of towel. Stitch along folded ends and upper edge of lace, using straight stitch. If upper edge of lace is unfinished or additional detailing is desired, cover the upper edge with a bias fabric band (page 117).

Embellishing with
Narrow Trims

MATERIALS

Purchased plain towel.

Narrow washable braid.

Water-soluble marking pen.

Fabric glue.

1 Preshrink trim, soaking in warm water; allow to dry. Transfer desired design to towel surface, using water-soluble marking pen.

Continued

Embellishing with
Narrow Trims
(continued)

2 Heat-set trim to follow intricate designs, using iron, if necessary. Apply liquid fray preventer to ends of trim; allow to dry. Glue-baste trim over design lines, turning under ½" (1.3 cm) at beginning and end.

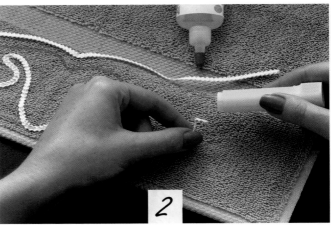

3 Thread machine, using upper thread that matches trim and bobbin thread that matches towel, or use monofilament nylon thread in both; attach open-toe embroidery foot, if available. Straight-stitch through center of narrow braids, backstitching at beginning and end.

Embellishing with
Reverse Appliqué

MATERIALS	
	Purchased plain towel.
	Washable mediumweight fabrics, such as polyester satin or taffeta, for the appliqué.
	Tear-away stabilizer.
	Machine embroidery thread in colors to match appliqué fabrics; regular thread to match towel.

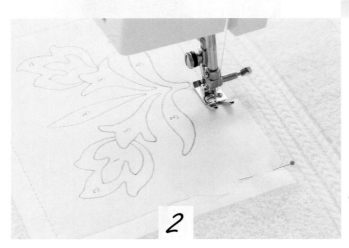

1 Trace the mirror image of appliqué design onto tear-away stabilizer. Number sections of design in the sequence they will be applied, beginning with those that should appear to be under other pieces. Cut the stabilizer at least 2" (5 cm) larger than the entire design.

2 Position tear-away stabilizer on wrong side of towel in the desired location. Baste in place.

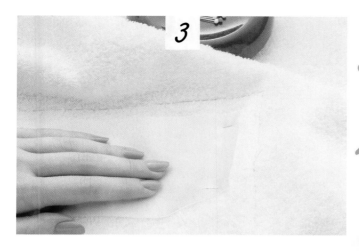

3 Cut the fabric for first piece to be applied, leaving ample margin around the shape. Pin in place, right side up, on right side of towel; insert pins from wrong side of towel, through stabilizer.

4 Stitch on design line for first shape, using short, straight stitches; use thread that matches towel.

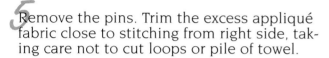

5 Remove the pins. Trim the excess appliqué fabric close to stitching from right side, taking care not to cut loops or pile of towel.

6 Repeat steps 3 to 5 for each piece in the appliqué, applying pieces in sequence as numbered in step 1.

7 Set the machine for closely spaced zigzag stitches; set the stitch width as desired. Loosen needle thread tension, if necessary, so the bobbin thread will not show on right side. Using thread that matches towel in the bobbin and thread that matches appliqué in needle, satin-stitch on design lines from right side; stitch sections in numbered sequence.

8 Remove tear-away stabilizer from wrong side of towel, taking care not to pull loops or pile of towel.

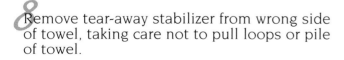

Scalloping & Binding a
Towel Edge

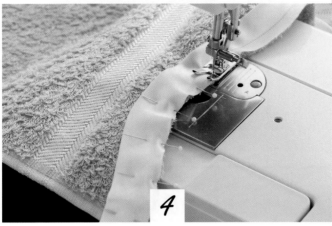

1 Make a pattern for the scalloped edge on tissue paper; plan for an odd number of gently curved scallops, with the depth of the scallops from the lowest to the highest point no more than 1" (2.5 cm). Pin pattern to towel in the desired location. Cut scalloped edge.

2 Cut 2" (5 cm) bias strip of fabric; piece strips together, if necessary, to make binding strip. Press strip in half lengthwise, wrong sides together, taking care not to distort width of the strip.

3 Pin binding strip to right side of towel, along scalloped edge, with the raw edges even; extend the binding ½" (1.3 cm) beyond sides of towel.

4 Stitch a scant ¼" (6 mm) from raw edges, easing the binding strip to fit curves of scallop.

5 Press the binding strip lightly toward lower edge. Fold ends of binding over the sides of towel; press. Wrap binding around the scalloped edge, and pin in the ditch of the seam.

6 Stitch in the ditch on the right side of the towel, catching binding on the wrong side of the towel.

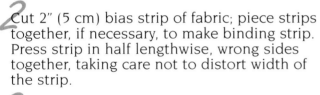

Adding a
Fabric Band to a Towel

MATERIALS

Purchased plain towel.

Washable mediumweight fabric, such as polyester satin or taffeta, for the band.

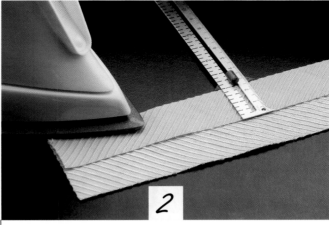

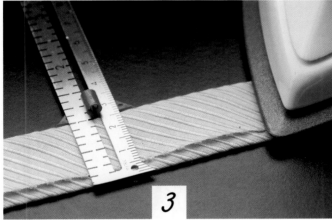

1 Cut a bias strip of the fabric, with cut width of strip ⅛" (3 mm) narrower than three times the desired finished width; cut the strip 1" (2.5 cm) longer than the width of towel.

2 Place fabric strip right side down on ironing surface. Press up an amount equal to desired finished width of band, taking care not to distort or stretch the fabric.

3 Press up opposite edge of fabric strip, so width between the pressed edges is equal to the finished width of the band, taking care not to distort fabric. On upper layer, raw edge does not meet the pressed edge.

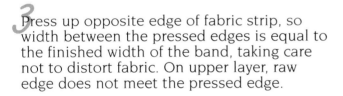

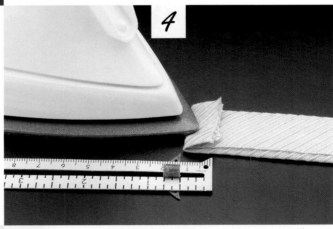

4 Press under ½" (1.3 cm) at ends of the bias strip, taking care not to distort or stretch fabric.

5 Pin bias fabric strip to towel in desired location. Stitch along outer edges of folded strip, stitching in the same direction on both sides; stitch ends.

Hamper Liner
LAUNDRY BAG

Hampers are great for collecting the laundry, but you still have to transport it to the laundry room. With the added weight of the hamper itself, that can be quite a chore. A decorative hamper liner that doubles as a laundry bag is a creative way to ease the load.

The bag is lined for added strength. Use the same fabric for the outside and lining. Or, select two coordinating fabrics, and sew a bag with a contrast casing. Designed to fit a rounded or rectangular hamper with a removable lid, the upper edge of the laundry bag folds down, exposing the lining, to form a 4" (10 cm) cuff.

MATERIALS

Mediumweight washable fabric for laundry bag and lining; amount determined by hamper size.

Strong cotton cording; circumference of hamper plus 45" (115 cm), optional.

Sew a drawstring tie (opposite) or use purchased cording as shown in the bag with a contrast casing (below and opposite).

Sewing a
Hamper Liner Laundry Bag

1 Cut fabric for laundry bag as determined in worksheet. Repeat for lining. Cut 2½" (6.5 cm) fabric strip for tie with length equal to circumference of hamper plus 45" (115 cm); seam pieces together, if necessary.

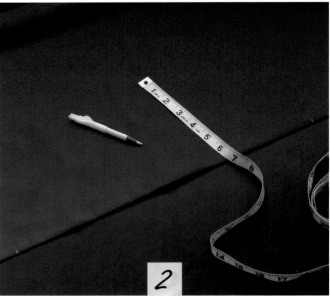

LAUNDRY BAG

<table>
<tr><td rowspan="17">W O R K S H E E T</td></tr>
</table>

Measure the circumference:	
Add 4" (10 cm) for ease.	+ 4"
Add 2" (5 cm) for seam allowances.	+ 2"
	=
Divide by 2	÷ 2
to find the cut width.	=
Measure inside height of hamper:	
Multiply by 2.	× 2
	=
Add longest diameter of bottom.	+
Add 8" (20.5 cm) for cuff.	+ 8"
Add 1" (2.5 cm) for seam allowances	+ 1"
to find total cut length.	=

2 Fold bag fabric in half crosswise, right sides together; press fold. Stitch ½" (1.3 cm) side seams; press open. Mark dots on fold equal distances from edges, with distance apart equal to longest hamper diameter.

3 Refold corners, so pressed fold aligns to side seams; pin. Draw lines through dots, perpendicular to fold.

4 Stitch on marked lines. Trim seam allowances to ½" (1.3 cm).

5 Repeat steps 2 to 4 for lining; leave 6" (15 cm) opening for turning near center of one side seam. Make a 1" (2.5 cm) buttonhole at center of one side, ⅝" (1.5 cm) from upper edge; reinforce with scrap of fusible interfacing on wrong side.

6 Slip lining inside outer bag, right sides together, aligning seams and upper edges; pin upper edges. Stitch ½" (1.3 cm) seam; press open.

7 Turn right side out through opening. Stitch opening closed. Press upper edge, centering seam.

Continued

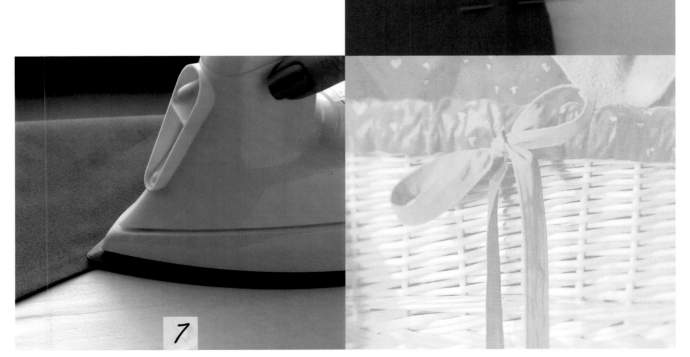

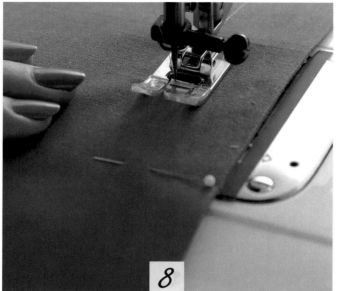

8

8 Stitch 1 1/4" (3.2 cm) from upper edge, forming casing. Omit step 9, if using purchased cording for drawstring.

9 Press under 1/4" (6 mm) on all edges of tie. Fold in half lengthwise, wrong sides together, aligning pressed folds; press. Stitch close to all edges.

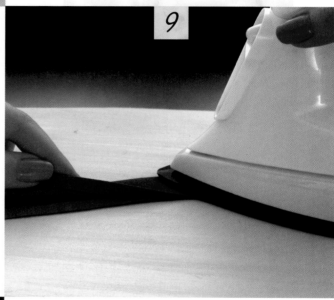

9

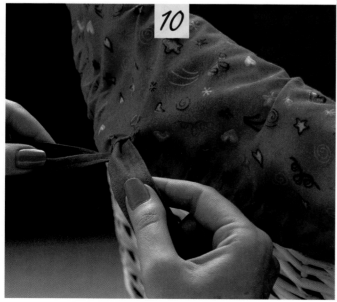

10

10 Insert drawstring through buttonhole, using bodkin or large safety pin. Place bag in hamper; fold upper edge over hamper top, forming cuff. Pull drawstring, easing cuff evenly.

Sewing a
Hamper Liner Laundry Bag
with a Contrast Casing

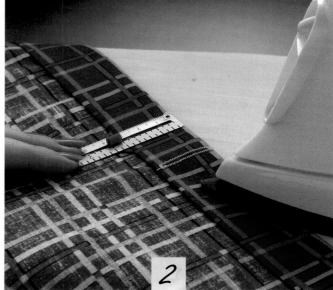

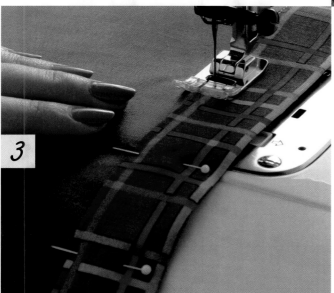

1 Cut bag and lining as on page 120, step 1, adding 3½" (9 cm) to cut length of outer bag. Follow steps 2 to 4 for bag and lining.

2 Make 1" (2.5 cm) buttonhole at center of one side of outer bag, ⅝" (1.5 cm) from upper edge; reinforce with scrap of fusible interfacing on wrong side. Press under ½" (1.3 cm) at top of outer bag. Press under again 1¼" (3.2 cm) from first foldline.

3 Insert lining into outer bag, wrong sides together, aligning seams. Slip upper raw edge of lining under folded upper edge of outer bag, aligning raw edge to foldline; pin. Stitch close to lower fold.

4 Insert purchased cording into casing. Or, make drawstring tie as in step 9, opposite. Finish as in step 10.

Working with
DECORATOR FABRICS

Decorator fabrics are designed with special char-
acteristics that make them more suitable than
fashion fabrics for large projects. They generally
come in wider widths: 48", 54", or 60" (122, 137, or
152.5 cm). Many are treated with stain-resistant
finishes because items like window curtains,
shower curtains, or pillow shams are not cleaned
as often as a garment would be.

Decorator fabrics with printed or woven designs
are printed or woven so that the pattern repeats
itself at regularly spaced intervals, both vertically
and horizontally. Also, when two widths of decorator fabric are sewn together just beyond the
selvages, the pattern can be matched perfectly,
making them ideal for large projects like duvet
covers and bedspreads.

Extra yardage is usually required for matching
patterned fabrics. After determining the cut length
needed, round this measurement up to the next
number divisible by the pattern repeat. Calculate
the total fabric needed by multiplying this adjusted cut length by the number of fabric widths
required; add one additional pattern repeat so
you can adjust the placement of the pattern on
the cut lengths. To have patterns match at the
seams, cut each length of fabric at the same point
on the pattern repeat. After seaming, trim to the
exact cut length needed.

Matching a
Patterned Fabric

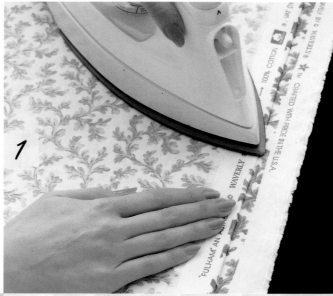

1

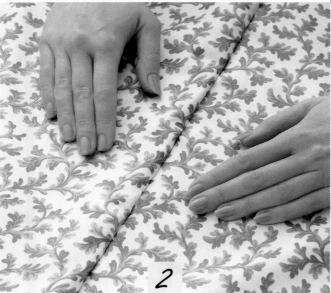

2

1 Position fabric widths right sides together, matching selvages. Fold back upper selvage until pattern matches; lightly press foldline.

2 Unfold selvage, and pin fabric widths together on foldline. Check the match from the right side.

3 Repin fabric so pins are perpendicular to foldline; stitch on foldline, using straight stitch. Trim away selvages; trim fabric to necessary cut length determined in project worksheet.

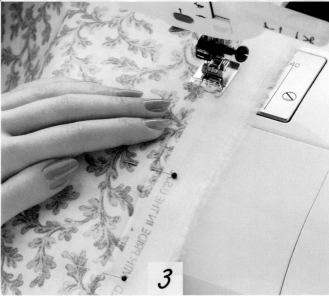

3

Index